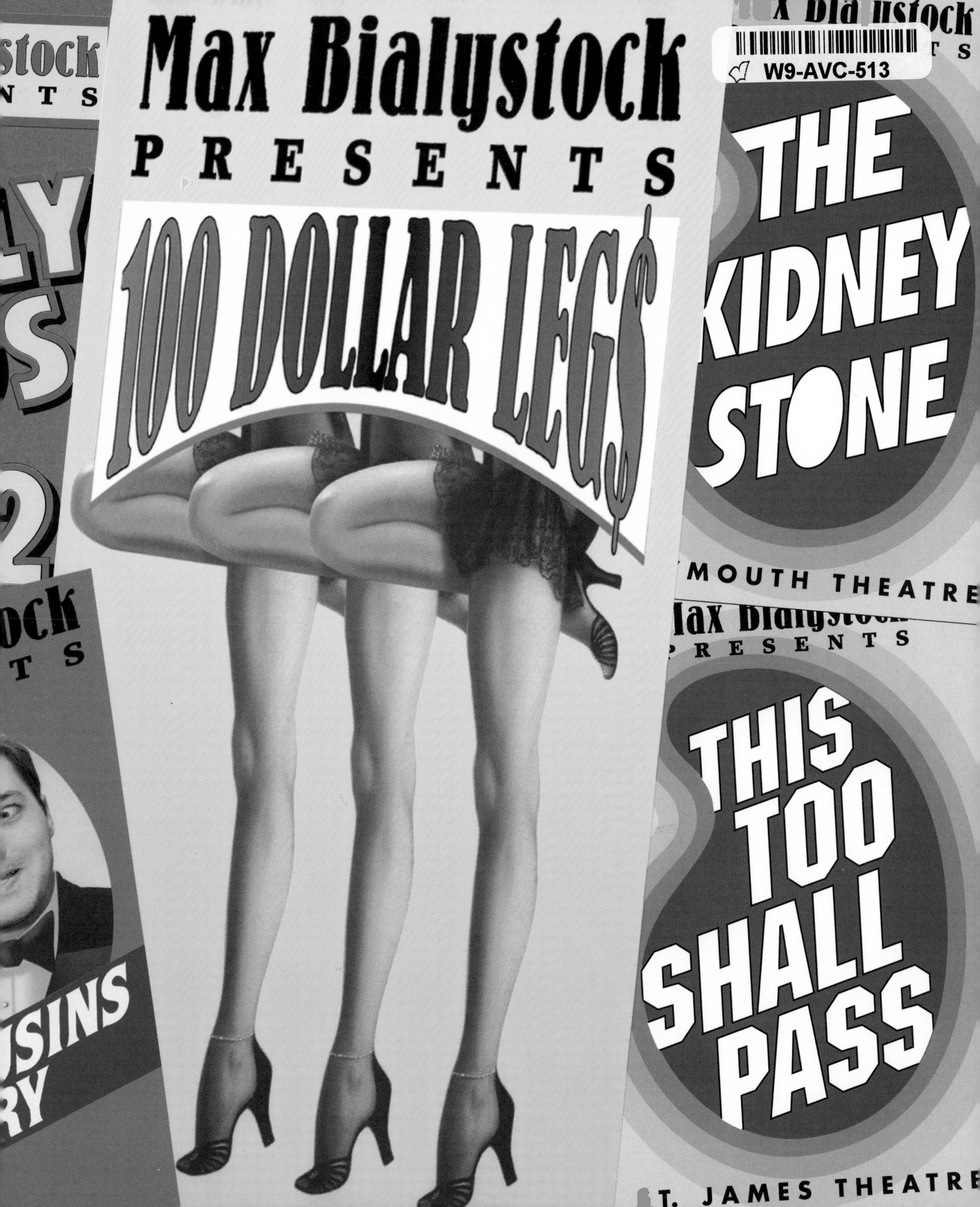
Max Bialystock
PRESENTS
100 DOLLAR LEG$
THE KIDNEY STONE
THIS TOO SHALL PASS

ST. JAMES THEATRE
246 WEST 44TH STREET
THE PRODUCERS
OPENING NIGHT
6:30 PM THU
APR 19

THE PRODUCERS

BY

MEL BROOKS

AND

TOM MEEHAN

PRINCIPAL PHOTOGRAPHY BY PAUL KOLNIK

A ROUNDTABLE PRESS BOOK

talk miramax books

HYPERION

A Roundtable Press Book
New York

talk miramax books

Special thanks to Actors Equity Association and the cast of *The Producers.*

Door logo courtesy of Serino Coyne, Inc.
Front cover image: Norman Jean Roy and Serino Coyne, Inc.
Back cover photograph: © 2001 Paul Kolnik
Author photograph: © 2001 Lyn Hughes

For Roundtable Press, Inc.
Directors: Marsha Melnick, Susan E. Meyer, Julie Merberg
Executive Editor: Patty Brown
Design: Joel Avirom, Jason Snyder, Meghan Day Healey
Editor: John Glenn
Editorial Assistant: Sara Newberry
Production: Bill Rose
Photographic Services: Michael Duggal, Duggal Visual Solutions

ISBN: 07868-6880-5
First Edition

2 4 6 8 10 9 7 5 3 1

ACKNOWLEDGMENTS

The authors, a.k.a. Mel and Tom, wish to warmly thank, from the bottom of our non-publishing-business hearts, all of those brilliant and incredibly hardworking publishing-business professionals who so skillfully and speedily put together this book. We wish to point extra-special fingers of thanks at Julie Merberg and Patty Brown, of Roundtable Press, and our genius, stay-up-all-night-to-get-the-job-done designers, Joel Avirom, Jason Snyder, and Meghan Day Healey.

And, of course, the book couldn't have happened at all without the total dedication of Talk Miramax Books' editorial director, JillEllyn Riley, a young woman of uncommon common sense, intelligence, patience, cheeriness, and highly developed people skills, especially in coping with a pair of grumpy no-longer-all-that-young men whom, she learned, absolutely had to have their tuna fish sandwiches on toasted rye, with no butter or mayonnaise, and a slice of tomato, no lettuce. Or else. We will miss our hours around the Talk Miramax Books conference table being goaded on to work by the lovely JillEllyn with her special treats of microwave popcorn and steaming cups of 100 percent Colombian coffee.

Finally, just to be on the safe side, we'd like to thank every man, woman, and child on the face of the earth, past, living, and yet to be born. And if that leaves any of you out, you have our deepest sympathy.

Where did we go right?

MAX AND LEO—ACT TWO, SCENE 5

PREFACE

ROCCO LANDESMAN

Would Mel Brooks be intolerable if he were not a genius? I guess this is a question for Anne Bancroft. The man, let's be honest, is not ego-free. When *The Producers* was in previews in Chicago, I went up to him after a performance and said, "You know, Mel, this is the funniest thing ever. And I mean *ever*, as in the history of comedy, going back to Aristophanes." He frowned. He looked vexed. What was going through his mind? Scenes from Marx Brothers movies? Molière? Chaplin? Finally, he said, "It's not funnier than *Blazing Saddles*."

So how did I fall in with such a character? I'm still not exactly sure. I do know that it was a cold April Sunday afternoon, big snowflakes in the air, and my wife, Debby, and I were grumpy because we had to come back early from the country. Mel's lawyer, Alan U. Schwartz, had arranged a reading.

Alan was there in the rehearsal room. So was Susan Stroman, who was directing; Mel and his co-bookwriter, Tom Meehan; the designers Robin Wagner and William Ivey Long; the actors Nathan Lane, Cady Huffman, and Gary Beach; and Anne Bancroft herself. Those, anyway, were the people I recognized. There were other important players in this project (like Glen Kelly, the musical supervisor), but I wouldn't get to know them until later. And there were about thirty other producers, each of whom, for better or worse, I knew.

I pretty much knew what to expect. *The Producers* had been a favorite movie of mine (but not as funny as, say . . . *Blazing Saddles*), and I expected a rather awkward first draft of an adaptation by someone with little (or certainly little recent) theatrical experience. I thought it might have its moments, but that I would say, "Promising. Show it to me again when you–pick one: (a) have a consistent point of view, (b) have a viable second act, (c) have some character development, (d) have a less confusing story line, or (e) have more funny lines and moments."

I couldn't have been more wrong. The reading began, and I started to laugh. Then I was laughing harder. Then I was actually crying. I don't cry in the theater. Haven't since I was twelve years old. Certainly not at readings. In fact, I don't tend to cry very much at all. So I'm crying, not at a tragedy, not even at a funeral, but at a goddamn *comedy*! We're five pages into the reading and tears are streaming down my cheeks. Debby later told me that Mel was watching me cry. Mel later told me that Anne was also. It was, I can't think of a better description, excruciatingly funny.

For about fifteen minutes my pleasure was pure and abandoned. But, with apologies to a certain movie director, where there is great pleasure there is also great . . . anxiety. My good friend Jerry Schoenfeld, head of the Shubert Organization (my good friend but also my competitor as a theater operator), was sitting almost next to me. The possibility of the funniest show ever written playing in a non-Jujamcyn house was very real. The reading, if anything, got funnier through the first act, and I was still laughing, but my anxiety level was getting noticeably higher.

What to do? I had made, by the end of the first act, an impulsive decision. My competitors might be bigger and stronger than I am, with more theaters and deeper pockets, but what does any athlete do in any sport when he might be overmatched? He makes up for what he lacks in size and power with the great equalizer: speed.

As the applause subsided at the end of Act One, I went straight to Mel and offered the St. James Theatre. Maybe the second act would be a letdown, but I'd take that chance. I even said to Mel, "The second act is going to have to be really bad to keep this from being a hit."

The second act was better, funnier than the first. The movie, which many, including myself, felt went flat after *Springtime for Hitler* becomes a hit, had been greatly improved by developing what had been just a seedling in the movie, the relationship between Max and Leo, into a real love story. Mel and Tom had not only made the story funnier but had added the decisive element of a human drama with an emotional payoff. In addition, the whole enterprise had been shaped (sometimes literally) as a valentine to Broadway, its ridicule cocooned in a deep and sustaining affection. And Stro's inspired staging, well, that would require another essay.

I've never produced a show where I've had so little to do with the creative process. Producers have egos, too, and we all want to be producers, not just presenters. If I had known how little influence I would have on this project, I would never have signed on, and given the joy that *The Producers* has been, every minute of every day, what a mistake that would have been! In Mel Brooks's world it snows in April, you cry at comedies, and big musical hits are virtually complete by the first reading. There's nothing I, or any of us, can do about it.

She had practiced it in her head several times. She read the number and dialed it, listened to it ring as nervous butterflies flew in her stomach. His father answered, putting him on the line. They found things to talk about, and talked for awhile about trips, "toiletries," and neighbors who talk to their garage. Suddenly, he had to get off the phone. "Wait!" and there she was, at the very moment in time she dreaded. "Um, will you go to the Sadie Hawkins dance with me?" Just the opposite of what she wanted. She said it in the little-girl voice she had tried to avoid. Too late. What would he say? Yes. Yes was the answer. And that was the beginning.

It was great. The nervous energy subsided after awhile. It was great. New jokes, new smiles, the first dance, the first hand hold. It was...grand. She felt special. But he didn't ask her out. She was perplexed. She thought he had a good time. Sunday, friends went to Silver Diner. She sat next to him. She felt wonderful. Perfect. But still nothing. She got sad. Everyone, including him, asked how she was. Finally, it happened. Tuesday night. They were a couple. She called her best friend, she told her mother. There was nothing she wanted more.

Months passed. The Relay for Life came, around the time of their second month together. A connection, a spark, a new closeness. Suddenly she was in a relationship. More jokes, studying for vocabulary, and tons of fun. They would be like this a long time. Other special events passed, other anniversaries. The summer was spent together, and they entered the following year as a couple. Things were still perfect. Homecoming, the fall play, and just normal things happened. His birthday arrived, and he was given a surprise party. She gave him two gifts. The student critic program for theatre provided more time for them to be together. They stayed as close as they could for as long as they could. The New Year rolled around, and time flew by. Suddenly, it was valentine's day, and they had been dating for eleven months. Slowly, the twelfth month arrived. Everything was perfect. Everything that happened in the past year was remarkable and something she had never experience before. She knew they would be together for a long time. Everything was all right as long as he was there.

"I hope you don't mind that I put down in words how wonderful life is now you're in the world"

"Seasons may change, winter to spring. But I love you, until the end of time."

"How do you measure a year?...Measure your life in love"

"But I die...without you"

"Are the stars out tonight? I don't know if it's cloudy or bright. I only have eyes for you"

"I'll know when my love comes along. I'll know then and there. I'll know at the sight of his face how I care, how I care, how I care"

"So please forgive this helpless haze I'm in, I've really never been in love before"

It's been a fantastic year. One of the best. I love you.

Amy Lerner

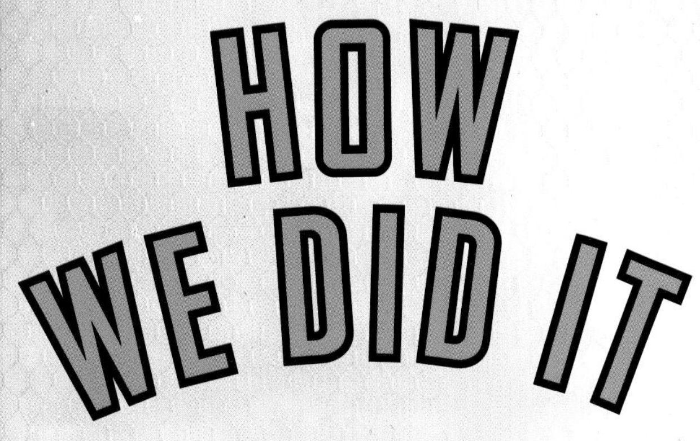

HOW WE DID IT

BY

MEL BROOKS

AND

TOM MEEHAN

Nervous Sunday • Geffen Calls • The Book • Searching for a Director • Bagel Mornings and Tuna Fish-and-Tomato-on-Rye-Toast Afternoons • A Go Show • Casting • Rehearsals • The Very Windy City • Opening Night

Tom Meehan and Mel Brooks

We may look as if we are deep in thought. We are actually contemplating where to go for lunch.

NERVOUS SUNDAY

APRIL 9, 2000 – TOM talks

We are pacing anxiously back and forth, Mel Brooks and I, one jittery Jew and one jumpy Irishman, looking like a pair of expectant fathers in a maternity-ward waiting room. Which, in a sense, we are. For our bouncing baby, also known as our musical adaptation of Mel's cult-classic 1968 film comedy, *The Producers*, is about to be presented for the first time ever in front of a real, live audience.

A baby is easy; it only takes nine months. But I've already been working with Mel Brooks on the book of *The Producers* for nearly two years, while he's been at it, writing the words and music for songs, for almost two and a half. We've spent countless hours—working at Mel's office and home in Los Angeles as well as in New York theatrical offices, apartments, and restaurants like Madame Romaine de Lyon (over omelets at a back table) and the Three Guys luncheonette (over tuna fish on rye toast with a slice of tomato, no lettuce, in the front booth, where one of the Three Guys often yelled at us, "C'mon, fellas, you been here over two hours, we need our booth back")—turning the movie into a musical.

The performance we're about to see, a so-called reading, is to be done by a company of a dozen highly accomplished Broadway actors led by Nathan Lane, the Tony Award-winning musical-comedy star, who has graciously agreed, along with the

Nathan Lane, one of the fastest wits in show business, once again breaks up Mel.

Mel Brooks and Anne Bancroft. The show looks good; their marriage is saved.

THE ORIGINAL ORIGINAL CAST
OF *THE PRODUCERS*

•••••

NOLA REHEARSAL STUDIO
STUDIO A – ELEVENTH FLOOR
250 WEST 54th STREET, NEW YORK, N.Y.
SUNDAY, APRIL 9, 2000 – 12:00 NOON

Narrated by Conrad John Schuck

Max Bialystock .... **NATHAN LANE***
Leopold Bloom .... **EVAN PAPPAS**
Franz Liebkind .... **NICK WYMAN**
Roger De Bris .... **GARY BEACH***
Carmen Ghia .... **MARIO CANTONE**
Ulla .... **CADY HUFFMAN***

Male ensemble and readers of male character roles:
GLENN RAINEY
ROB LOREY
JERRY DIXON
GORDON STANLEY

Female ensemble and readers of female character roles:
KEESHA FLETH SHARP
JENNIFER SMITH*
JOAN BARBER
DENISE NOLAN

***Later a member of the Broadway cast of* The Producers**

others, to do our reading for the princely sum of $0.00. We are worried that, among others, Nathan won't like the show. He is our first and only choice to play the leading role in the musical, the part of the down-on-his-luck Broadway producer Max Bialystock, portrayed so memorably in the film by Zero Mostel.

Furthermore, heightening our anxiety up to somewhere around total panic, Nathan and the others are going to be doing the show for what we figure is probably the world's toughest audience—a pitiless, poker-faced gathering of approximately fifty of Broadway's most prominent theater owners, producers, and deep-pocket investors.

It is nearly noon on a chilly, overcast, midtown Manhattan Sunday morning in early April. From the eleventh-floor window of the Nola Rehearsal Studio, a famed if somewhat dingy and beat-up suite of rehearsal rooms in a nondescript office building on West 54th Street, we look out to see that, even though it is spring, heavy, fat snowflakes have begun to fall on the bleak city. We overhear a couple of burly workmen pushing a baby-grand piano into our rehearsal room, Studio A. "Uh-oh, snow in April," one of them says to the other. "Not a good omen."

Now the members of our audience begin arriving, shivering, briskly brushing snow from their coats, and looking not in the least pleased to have been dragged out into a blizzard, on a Sunday of all days, to go through the polite ritual of sitting through a reading of a new musical—something they've probably had to endure at least twenty times this season. Mel and I greet each of the arrivals with cheery hellos and our most ingratiating smiles but get little in return.

Thank God, there are a few sympathetic faces in the gathering crowd, like Mel's lawyer, Alan U. Schwartz; Mel's friends Bob and Laura Sillerman; Mel's cousin, Howard Kaminsky, a leading editor who is well known in New York book-publishing circles; and especially our wives, Mrs. Thomas Meehan, a.k.a. Carolyn Capstick, the spirited and forever-smiling blonde Greenwich Village entrepreneur, and Mrs. Mel Brooks, a.k.a. Anne Bancroft, the celebrated Tony and Academy Award–winning stage and film actress. They couldn't be cheerier or more supportive, although Anne quickly alerts us, "I've resolved not to be a shill for you guys and laugh my head off so that these producers will think it's good and want to put it on Broadway. I'm sorry, but I'm that kind of person. So if you notice that I'm not laughing, that's why. Although I'm sure it's going to be very funny." "Okay, I resolve not to laugh, either," adds Carolyn. We warmly thank them for their resolve.

High noon. Mel and I step outside as the audience takes its place in the cramped rehearsal hall. They settle into three rows of fifteen or so metal folding chairs per row facing a dozen music stands, behind each of which is a stool that a cast member is about to perch on while reading from the script and singing. Nothing has been memorized—the actors, recruited by Broadway's leading casting agency, Johnson-Liff Associates, have had only a few days to learn the songs and to do a couple of quick cold readings of the book. No scenery, no props, no costumes, no lights. No hope? We hope not.

Tom, Mel, Susan Stroman, and Glen Kelly at the piano

Led by Nathan Lane, the cast enters Studio A, and the door is closed. The reading is about to begin. "What have we got to be worried about?" we say, shake hands, and start to enter. But then we stop and stare at one another. *What have we got to be worried about?* Plenty! We've taken *The Producers*, for which Mel won the Academy Award in 1968 for Best Original Screenplay, and changed it from start to finish. We've put in a new beginning and a new ending; we've cut entire scenes and lines that devoted fans of the film have been laughing at for over thirty years; and we've even had the nerve to write brand-new scenes that hadn't been in the movie, along with scores of brand-new lines. Moreover, as the lyricist and composer of the show's score, Mel has stuck no fewer than sixteen brand-new songs into *The Producers*, to go with the two he'd already written for the movie, "Springtime for Hitler" and "Prisoners of Love." What a monumental display of unabashed chutzpah! We know that God and the *New York Times* will surely punish us for our transgressions.

Our sweet-tempered and tireless young stage manager, Elaine Baylis, sticks her head out the door and informs us that everyone is waiting for us. We have to face the music. Literally. We slink into the room and take a couple of seats in the back row at the far end, next to the piano, at which sits our resident-genius musical supervisor, Glen

Nathan as "The King of Broadway" in rehearsal— "It's good to be the king!"

Kelly, a boyish-looking redhead in his early thirties who has a fixed smile on his face, betraying a high degree of high anxiety.

On the other side of the piano stands someone who doesn't seem to be nervous at all: our bright-eyed and beautiful director/choreographer, Susan Stroman, chipper and upbeat, as always, dressed in her trademark black pants and jacket, topped inevitably by a black baseball cap, out of the back of which sticks a perky blonde ponytail. Stro, as she is known to one and all, is even happily grinning as she steps forward to introduce the cast to the audience and to explain to them that they are about to hear the world-premiere reading of the musical version of *The Producers*. We're hoping to go to Broadway and are looking for only three things: a producer, a theater, and $10 million. "Smile, laugh if you want to, and have a good time," says Stro cheerfully.

The music begins. Mel and I wink at each other in terror. Now, as the music modulates quietly, our narrator, Conrad John Schuck—a friend and veteran stage, film, and TV actor—sets the scene. "Shubert Alley," he reads, "on an early spring night in 1959. The audience is coming out of the Shubert Theatre after seeing the opening-night performance of Max Bialystock's latest show, *Funny Boy,* a new musical version of *Hamlet*." Laughter. Not loud laughter. But definitely a little bit of laughter. Mel shrugs, I shrug. It means nothing. Our chorus of four men and four women belts out "Opening Night," a bright, upbeat curtain-raiser about how much they hated *Funny Boy* and have nothing but contempt for its producer, Max Bialystock. The number gets a couple of little laughs and polite applause. Anyway, nobody gets up and walks out.

Now, all eyes turn to Nathan Lane, as Max Bialystock entering Shubert Alley in the midst of reading the *New York Times* on the subject of *Funny Boy*. Here we go. Baby's first jokes. "The reviews come out a lot faster," says Nathan, "when the critics leave at intermission." And, "By the end of *Funny Boy,* Max Bialystock's hopeless musical of *Hamlet,* everybody is dead. They were the lucky ones." Laughter. Real laughter. Loud laughter. Everyone in the room is laughing, led by Anne Bancroft and Carolyn Capstick. So much for resolve. Next, Nathan launches into his opening number, "The King of Broadway," a mournful Russian-Jewish-Gypsy–style lament that gradually picks up speed and finally comes to a lunatic, up-

Cady Huffman: One of the big reasons Tom loved working on The Producers.

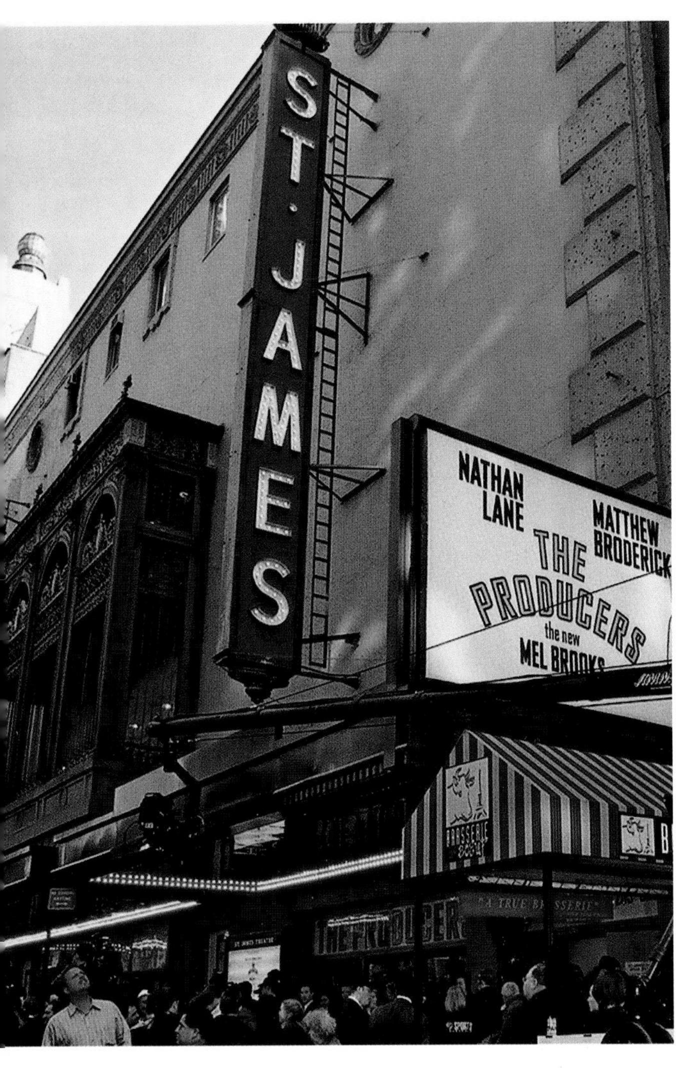

tempo, Danny Kaye–like finish, a cascading tongue-twister of nearly a dozen classic Mel Brooks lines that each rhymes with "nights again"—"lights again," "brights again," "kites again," "slights again," "delights again," "plights again," "blights again," "frights again," "sights again," "flights again," and "heights again." When Nathan breathlessly finishes the number, Studio A breaks out in a storm of cheers and applause. Nathan has stopped the show three minutes after it has started. Mel leans over to me and, quoting Gene Wilder in *Young Frankenstein,* whispers, "It . . . could . . . work."

The reading continues. And so does the laughter at virtually every joke in the script—laughs at old lines from the movie as well as at new ones. Next, about half an hour into the reading, Gary Beach—as Broadway's worst director, the effetely flamboyant Roger De Bris—comes onto the scene, and the reading is once again stopped cold when he leads our male chorus in "Keep It Gay," a tongue-in-cheek celebration of the gay life that both Mel and I had feared might get rocks thrown at us by audiences but is instead happily embraced and greeted by roars of laughter. And only moments later, the reading is stopped cold for a third time by the very tall, very blonde, and very gorgeous Cady Huffman, as the Swedish bombshell Ulla, when she belts out "When You Got It, Flaunt It!" As the applause for Cady goes on and on, Mel's cousin, Howard, steps over and whispers in his ear. "First thing tomorrow morning," he says, "I'm going to Abercrombie & Fitch and buy a pick-ax, pitons, and a thousand feet of very strong rope." Mel looks at him, puzzled. "What for?" Howard replies with a big grin, "I'm going to climb Cady Huffman."

End of Act One. Intermission. Mel and I are standing next to one another in a corner by the piano, bewildered and slightly shell-shocked, when a ruddy-faced, broadly smiling gentleman pushes his way through the crowd to us. He is none other than Rocco Landesman, debonair bon vivant and theater highbrow who'd once taught at the Yale School of Drama, legendarily successful horse-racing devotee, and, most significant, president since 1987 of the Jujamcyn Theatre Group, the owner of several of Broadway's most prestigious theaters. "I love it, absolutely love it," says Rocco, enthusiastically over-the-top. "If you want the St. James, you can have the St. James!"

The St. James? One of the three or four most sought-after musical theaters in all of New York. Shows have waited for years to get a chance to play the St. James. *Oklahoma!* had opened at the St. James, and so had *The King and I* and *Hello, Dolly!* The St. James is a landmark, a legend. And now, *at the intermission* of our very first reading, we've been offered the St. James? This is fictional, something that happens in movies, not in real life.

The reading of Act Two, featuring Gary Beach leading "Springtime for Hitler," amazingly goes even better than Act One. Either these people are dumb or we've seriously underestimated our show. And they don't look dumb. As the last of the audience is filing noisily and happily out of Studio A, Mel and I stand side by side with foolish grins on our faces, accepting congratulations from a very happy Glen Kelly and an even happier Susan Stroman. "Guys," she says, giving each of us a big hug, "I think you've got yourselves a musical." And Gary Beach, as he is leaving, cries out to us, "Mel, Tom, it's a hit! You've got yourselves a great big hit!"

A hit? We've got ourselves a hit? Mel and I are walking on air, but a few minutes later we quickly come crashing back down to earth again. A hit? Are we crazy? We've heard the show read once for a relative handful of Broadway insiders who admittedly seemed to love it. But that scarcely makes it a hit. "Never go by audiences that include family and friends, especially audiences that haven't paid to get in—that's one of the cardinal rules of the theater," I tell Mel.

Furthermore, despite all the laughter, we saw that the second half of Act Two—especially the scenes immediately following "Springtime for Hitler"—was far too long and needed to be seriously cut. Also, are we out of our minds? We're hoping to sign up a cast led by Nathan Lane, one of the most brilliantly talented actors and singers in the history of American musical comedy, and where will he be during "Springtime for Hitler," the show's biggest production number? Backstage playing pinochle with a bunch of stagehands, because he isn't in "Springtime for Hitler"! We have to write a great, old-fashioned, knock-'em-in-the-aisles, stop-the-show eleven-o'clock number for Nathan sometime late in Act Two. We? I at once hand that little task over to our composer/lyricist, Mel Brooks.

"First thing tommorow morning, I'm going to Abercrombie & Fitch and buy a pick-ax, pitons, and a thousand feet of very strong rope . . . . I'm going to climb Cady Huffman."

—Howard Kaminsky, leading New York publishing executive and Mel's cousin

And all those producers and moneymen who laughed all afternoon long. "Are we kidding ourselves?" I say. "We'll probably never hear from any of them ever again." "You're right," agrees Mel. What have we got to worry about? Plenty! We look out the window. The snow has stopped, and the sun has come brilliantly out in a cloudless azure sky. Mel shrugs, I shrug. A gorgeous sunshiny afternoon to top off our world-premiere Sunday. Could that mean anything? The same two burly workmen pass by, wheeling our piano out of Studio A. "Uh-oh, sunshine after snowfall in April," says one of them to the other. "Not a good omen."

Uh-oh. Maybe we shouldn't have written this musical in the first place. A fine Laurel-and-Hardy mess we've gotten ourselves into! How did it all happen, Mel, how?

GEFFEN CALLS

SPRING, 1998 – MEL talks

How did it happen? I'll tell you how it happened.

Two years earlier, in April 1998, I was sitting in my office at the Culver Studios in Los Angeles. Shortly before noon, my fiercely loyal and incredibly hard-working executive assistant of nearly twenty years, the lovely Leah Zappy, stuck her head into my office to tell me that I had a gentleman caller on line 1. "Whoever it is, I don't care if it's the pope or the president," I emphatically told her, "I'm busy, I can't talk, I'm not here." "It's David Geffen," she said. "I'm not busy, I can talk, I'm here, put him on," I said.

David Geffen, in case the name is unfamiliar to you, is a more than slightly well-off record-industry legend who, in partnership with Steven Spielberg and Jeffrey Katzenberg, had in 1995 founded DreamWorks SKG, Hollywood's newest major movie studio. David is a very important man. There is no one in Hollywood who wouldn't take his calls. Especially including me, not only because of his enormous power but also because I happen to be very fond of him. He is one of the wittiest and most charming men in all show business, as well as one of the smartest.

Why had he called? David had an idea. He would produce and I would write a Broadway musical version of *The Producers*. Was I interested? I thought about it for a moment. David was famous for his unerring ability to sense potential big-time commercial success. He also knew the Broadway musical theater, having been the original New York producer, along with the Shuberts, of no less a mega-hit than *Cats*. In addition, as both producer and the man who'd come up with the title, he'd been a critically important contributor to the Broadway success of Michael Bennett's *Dreamgirls*. So if someone as super-smart as David Geffen thought that a musical version of *The Producers* was a good idea, who was I to tell him no? Mel Brooks! "No!" I shouted into the phone. "It's a perfectly good movie. Let's leave it as it is." And that was that. Or so I thought as I hung up the phone.

Actually, over the years a number of others, including well-known Broadway producers like Alexander Cohen, had approached me with the idea of turning *The Producers* into a musical, and I'd given each of them a polite but definite no.

Early the next morning, Leah again stuck her head into my office. Guess who was on the line, again? I took David's call, of course. Once again, he urged me at length to do the musical, and once again, at short length, I gave him my usual polite no. But David, I was soon to learn, does not take no for an answer, polite or otherwise, and for something like the next three weeks it seemed as though he was on the phone almost every twenty minutes giving me another sales talk on why I should do the musical.

I began to weaken. All my life, ever since the age of nine, when my Uncle Joe took me to my first Broadway show, Cole Porter's *Anything Goes*, I'd had the not-so-secret desire to be a Broadway composer/lyricist, like Porter or Irving Berlin. And over the years I'd written a whole bunch of songs for my movies. Lyrics came easily to me, and while I'd had absolutely no formal musical training, I'd worked out a way of composing music by picking out tunes I heard in my head on a piano, singing them into a tape recorder, and then having a musicologist transcribe them into actual notes on actual music paper. What if, I thought, David Geffen would agree to let me write the score for the musical? Now, that would be really exciting, and I just might do it.

I excitedly called David with this idea but found him to be somewhat less than enthusiastic. He already had a songwriter in mind for *The Producers*, with whom he'd already discussed the project. The songwriter was none other than Jerry Herman, who had expressed strong interest in doing the show. I could scarcely argue that I was a better songwriter than Jerry, whose words and music I'd cheered for over the years in one memorable smash-hit musical after another, among them *Hello, Dolly!, Mame,* and *La Cage aux Folles.* So, slightly bewildered, somehow now finding myself having been talked by David into writing only the book of the musical, I agreed to meet with Jerry to talk over the show.

I went to his home in Beverly Hills, where he led me into his music room and immediately surprised me with the news that he wasn't going to do *The Producers* because he didn't feel that he was the right man. "But David assured me that you were all set to write the score," I said. "I'm mad for David Geffen," said Jerry, "but he does have this one little quirk: He doesn't seem to know how to take no for an answer." Ah, yes, I thought, that would be the same David Geffen that I know and love. "I never told him yes," Jerry went on, "because the first time he called I instantly thought of another songwriter who would be absolutely perfect for the job."

"Who is he?" I asked.

"I'll play you a couple of his songs," said Jerry, settling at his grand piano and first playing "I'm Tired," a parody of a Marlene Dietrich song that the unforgettable Madeline Kahn had sung in *Blazing Saddles*, and then "Hope for the Best, Expect the Worst," which was from my second movie, *The Twelve Chairs.*

"Hey, hold on a minute," I said to Jerry. "I wrote those songs."

"Of course you did. I know and admire all of your songs. You happen to be a very good songwriter."

"I am?" I asked.

"You are," he said. "And furthermore, you'd be nuts to do a Broadway musical of *The Producers* without including 'Springtime for Hitler' and 'Prisoners of Love.' Two of your major songs are already written. All you need is a few more and you'll have yourself a full score. Go, with my blessings, and do it!"

With some slight reluctance, David Geffen gave in. "All right," he said. "If Jerry says you can and you think you can, too, let's at least give it a try." And so in early June 1998 I sat down to write the first of what would turn out to be seventeen new songs I would eventually write for the musical. Actually, I wasn't at first sure where to begin. But then I thought of a line from the movie spoken by Max Bialystock soon after the shocking success of *Springtime for Hitler* has put him and Leopold Bloom in serious jeopardy of landing in jail: "Where did we go right?" It sounded like a song to me, and in fact a tune quickly popped into my head. Within a couple of days I had a fairly complete set of lyrics—later many times to be revised—written in longhand on a yellow legal pad. "The show was lousy and long," I remember beginning. "We did everything wrong,/ Where did we go right?" And those first lines actually made it all the way to the St. James. Anyway, on or about the sixth of June 1998, I'd made the first tentative and tiny baby steps toward turning *The Producers* into a musical.

THE BOOK

•••••••

LATE SUMMER, 1998 – TOM talks

If you take a nine a.m. plane from New York to Los Angeles, the six-hour flight, with the three-hour time difference, gets you into L.A. at exactly noon, leaving enough time to pick up your luggage, grab a cab, and make it to the Culver Studios, in Culver City, just in time for a one o'clock appointment. Which is exactly what I did a couple of days after Labor Day 1998 to meet with a pair of longtime friends and writing partners, Mel Brooks and Ronny Graham.

The main purpose of my trip to California was to talk over a tentative offer that the three of us had from MGM to write a sequel to a movie that we'd written together in the mid-1980s, *Spaceballs*, an off-the-wall parody of the *Star Wars* movies that MGM had released with great success in 1986. I was somewhat interested in the project only because it presented an opportunity to work again with Mel and Ronny, for we'd had a riotously wacky time doing *Spaceballs*, as well as *To Be or Not to Be*, another of Mel's pictures that we'd done earlier. Within minutes of my meeting with my old partners, however, Mel got a phone call from a top executive at MGM with the dismaying news that the studio wanted to make the *Spaceballs* sequel as an animated film rather than live action. "Forget it," we told MGM. "We don't do cartoons." *Spaceballs 2* was not to be, but another and far more exciting project immediately raised its intriguing head.

"That face, that face, that glorious face . . ." Mel, we never realized, you're a good singer!

Along with his many other talents, Ronny Graham was an accomplished pianist, and as we were about to end our meeting in Mel's office, Mel turned to Ronny and asked him to play some songs he wanted me to hear on the office piano. Ronny smiled, sat down at the upright, and began playing and singing "Where Did We Go Right?" which, unbeknownst to me at the time, was the first song that Mel had written for his score of *The Producers*.

"It's funny, I like it," I said, puzzled, when Ronny had finished singing. "But what is it?"

Mel filled me in. Since June, he'd been working on songs for a Broadway musical version of *The Producers*, and he had now finished drafts of three of them.

"I think Mel's songs are great," said Ronny enthusiastically. "He's a natural, like his idols, Irving Berlin and Cole Porter."

"Ronny has been my biggest cheerleader ever since I started writing the songs," said Mel. "In fact, I might even have given up if it hadn't been for his constant encouragement. But now, actually, I think they're pretty good myself."*

Once I'd gotten Ronny to play and sing all three of them, I suggested that Mel's songs were a lot more than pretty good. They were *very* good—tuneful, upbeat, funny when they were meant to be funny and also touching when they were meant to be touching, reminding me of songs from some of the great Broadway musical comedies of the 1940s and 1950s, like *Where's Charley?, High Button Shoes*, and *Guys and Dolls*.

Now that he had written his new songs to go along with "Springtime for Hitler" and "Prisoners of Love," said Mel, he felt more or less confident that he could do an

*A sad note: Ronny Graham, who had been one of Mel's closest friends since they collaborated on *New Faces of 1952*, died in the spring of 1999 at the age of seventy-nine. No one would have been happier about the Broadway success of *The Producers*.

entire Broadway score and so was ready to start writing the book. "But I don't want to write it alone," he said, "because who knows where it should sing and where it should talk." He needed someone to collaborate with on the book, someone who had made a specialty of writing the books for musicals. "In other words, Tommy me boy, *you*," he said. "You wrote the book for *Annie* and won the Tony, so you must know what you're doing."

"You want me to be your collaborator on the book for *The Producers*?" I asked.

"Yes," he said.

"Do it!" said Ronny excitedly.

"I'll do it!" I quickly cried out before Mel could change his mind. I hadn't been more excited and enthusiastic about anything that had come my way in years. As a writer of musical books, I like to think that I know a good idea for a musical when I hear one, and a musical based on *The Producers* was one of the best I'd ever heard. The movie itself was already partly a musical, featuring one of the funniest musical numbers ever put on film, "Springtime for Hitler," which I sensed could be at least as funny on the stage.

Of course, I pointed out to Mel, there were plenty of problems to be faced in turning *The Producers* into a musical, just as there are in turning any movie into a work for the stage, because movies and musicals are constructed in entirely different ways.

"What we've got to do," I told Mel later that afternoon, after Ronny had left and we'd sat down for our first work session, "is to take the screenplay of *The Producers* entirely apart, as though we are disassembling the works of a finely crafted Swiss watch, and then put it back together again, adding new pieces where necessary, taking out old pieces that no longer fit the new construction, and end up with it still ticking. Or to switch to another metaphor, turning the screenplay of *The Producers* into the musical book of *The Producers* will be not unlike trying to translate it from English into Serbo-Croatian."

"In other words," said Mel, "it's going to be a very hard job."

"Yes," I said.

"Thanks, I already knew that," said Mel. "Get out one of your yellow legal pads, I'll talk, and we'll start trying to outline the show. And for God's sake, please, no more metaphors." Our collaboration had begun.

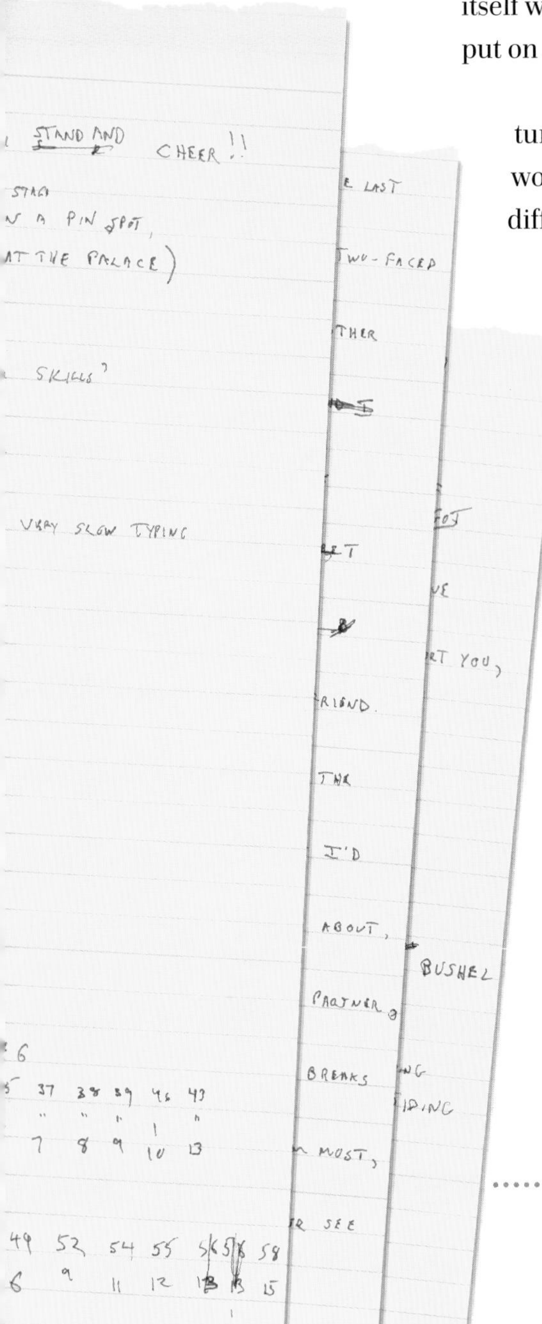

SEARCHING FOR A DIRECTOR

LATE NOVEMBER 1998 & ONWARD - MEL talks

I walked smack into the middle of Mr. Fezziwig's boisterous Christmas ball. Where was I? In a large rehearsal hall upstairs in the Ford Center for the Performing Arts, a theater on 42nd Street in New York, where an exuberant cast was doing a run-through of a musical version of Dickens's *A Christmas Carol.* The rehearsal abruptly stopped and all turned to gaze at me in bewilderment. Why had Mel Brooks, of all unlikely people, walked into the room?

Why indeed? I'll tell you why. Because we were looking for a director. But not just any director. It had to be someone with a real flair for what has become all but a lost art, directing not simply a musical but an old-fashioned musical comedy. For that's what we wanted *The Producers* to be. Years ago, the musical comedy had been a staple of the New York theater. For a forty-year period beginning around the end of World War I, at least three or four brand-new ones turned up on Broadway each season. But for some reason, along about 1960, the musical comedy went out of vogue, became

passé, and for the last forty years only a handful, mainly revivals, have made it to town. Unhappily, as far as I'm concerned, the musical comedy was replaced by what might be called the musical tragedy, the kind of show, often from London, in which you sit in the dark all evening long without laughing once. And though you stopped smoking years ago, because you knew that smoking causes cancer, you long throughout the entire show for a Lucky Strike.

So, since musical comedies are rarely done anymore, it's difficult to find anyone who knows how to direct them, especially since Broadway's greatest all-time musical comedy director, George Abbott, passed away a few years ago, struck down and cruelly taken from us at the tender age of 107. Who could we find to direct *The Producers*?

I first met Mel in November 1998 with my husband, director Mike Ockrent. We opened the door to our New York apartment and there stood the legendary Mel Brooks, singing in full voice the song "That Face," which now opens the second act of The Producers. *He passed right by us, singing and dancing down our long hallway. He finished the song with a big "Brooksian" jeté onto the living room sofa! Then he said, "Hello, I'm Mel Brooks." We were enamored immediately. Mel had come to us for help in transforming his Academy Award–winning screenplay* The Producers *into a musical comedy.*

—Susan Stroman

Tom had had an idea. He suggested Mike Ockrent, a British director now living in New York who'd directed a pair of big, old-fashioned musical comedies, *Me and My Girl* and *Crazy for You*, which had been big hits in the early and mid-1990s in both London and New York. He is very good with comedy, Tom said.

"I know, I saw them both," I told him, "and I thought that they were both terrific, very well staged and with plenty of laughs. Maybe Ockrent could be our guy."

"And if he is," Tom told me, "he comes with an extra added attraction. His wife, who works with him on almost all of his musicals, is just about the best choreographer in town, and so we might be able to get her to do *The Producers*, too."

"His wife, huh?" I said. "What's her name?"

"Susan Stroman," he said.

I was on the phone in Los Angeles talking to Tom in New York. "Ockrent and Stroman," I said. "Find them and set up a meeting for all four of us when I fly into New York next week."

He found them. They were in the midst of rehearsals for their fourth annual production of *A Christmas Carol*. And through their agent, Tom scheduled our Ford Center meeting for the afternoon after I'd arrived in New York. But when I got to town early the night before, I decided to do a crazy thing. I went up to Ockrent and Stroman's West 57th Street penthouse apartment for a surprise visit. Unannounced and unexpected, I walked in their door dancing and singing my favorite song, "That Face," words and music by Mel Brooks, from my favorite unwritten Broadway musical, *The Producers*. They were taken aback, to say the least, when I went dancing down their long hall into their living room, where I finished the number standing on their sofa. "Hello, I'm Mel Brooks," I said.

"Hello," they said. They seemed to like "That Face" and my face, and I found in return that I also liked theirs. We spent only a few minutes together, but, to quote the opening line of *Catch-22*, by my longtime friend the late Joseph Heller, "It was love at first sight."

But back to the Ford Center. Ockrent, a smiling Englishman in his early fifties, handsome, winningly charming from the first moment you met him, gave the cast a twenty-minute break and escorted me—along with Tom, plus Stro, as we would soon come to know her, and Glen Kelly, the dance arranger for *A Christmas Carol*, who would become a close personal friend and a major contributor to *The Producers* as its musical supervisor and dance arranger—into a small private room across the hall, where we all sat down to talk about how you go about making a movie into a musical comedy.

To begin with, Mike made it known, he, Stro, and Glen were crazy about the movie and had seen it many, many times. Mike was thrilled, he said, to be considered for the job and would be available to begin working on it within two or three months. Furthermore, having heard about the possibility of becoming involved with the musical, he and Stro were already bubbling with ideas about how to put the movie on the stage. In addition, Mike offered, if I was in need of a master musician to assist me in putting my music down on paper and arranging it, Glen Kelly was eagerly ready, wildly willing, and surpassingly able to take on the job.

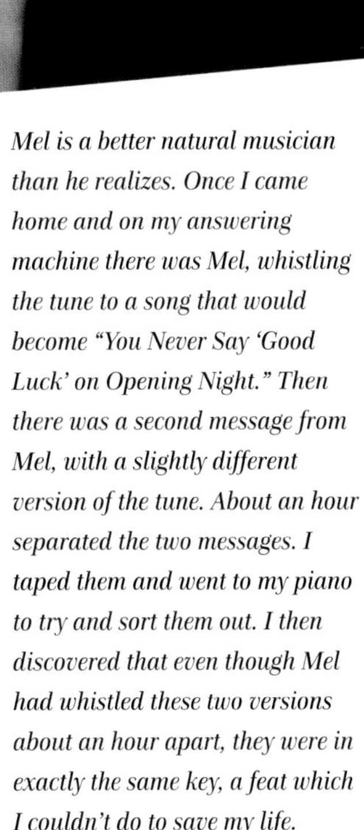

Mel is a better natural musician than he realizes. Once I came home and on my answering machine there was Mel, whistling the tune to a song that would become "You Never Say 'Good Luck' on Opening Night." Then there was a second message from Mel, with a slightly different version of the tune. About an hour separated the two messages. I taped them and went to my piano to try and sort them out. I then discovered that even though Mel had whistled these two versions about an hour apart, they were in exactly the same key, a feat which I couldn't do to save my life.

—Glen Kelly

A half-hour later, when Tom and I left the Ford Center, we looked at one another and nodded. We knew immediately that we had struck gold in finding Mike, Stro, and Glen—a director, a choreographer, and a musical supervisor, three of the most critical jobs in the creation of a musical, and we seemed to have found the ideal trio to take on the jobs in the twinkling of a twenty-minute rehearsal break. They were soon committed to the project, and we couldn't have been more fortunate to get them.

Nobody, however, was quite ready to start working full-time on *The Producers*. In fact, earlier commitments separated all of us for several months, and Tom and I didn't get around to start actually turning out the book until early spring. In the meantime, Tom had gone off with Carolyn to spend the month of February 1999 on a remote and exceedingly unfashionable Caribbean island. He brought along his computer, a copy of *The Producers* screenplay, and all the lyrics I'd written so far. He took it upon himself to crash through a rough draft of the entire musical, spewing it out in twenty-eight days. It was a hefty, 175-page kitchen-sink document that included drafts of all kinds of ideas we'd talked about, like a ten-page scene that took place at an outdoor seaside nightclub

in Rio and featured a song I'd written, destined for the scrap heap, entitled "You'll Find Your Happiness in Rio." It contained this immortal verse:

You'll find your happiness in Rio,
The beaches there are strewn with pearls,
The tropic breezes always blow there,
And so, I hear, do the girls!

In early March, when Tom got back to New York, he phoned Mike Ockrent to tell him that he'd like to drop off the script. A secretary answered, however, and gave Tom another number where he could reach Mike. Tom assumed that the second number was most likely a rehearsal hall or a production office, but when he called he was dismayed to find that it was the number of a private room in Memorial Sloan-Kettering Cancer Center, New York's leading hospital for the treatment of cancer, and that the patient in the room was Mike himself. We learned that Mike had leukemia and was in Sloan-Kettering to be prepped for a bone-marrow transplant that, if successful, his doctors assured him, would leave him permanently cured. I soon came east to New York, to begin working full-time with Tom and Glen on *The Producers,* and we went to Sloan-Kettering to visit Mike several times. He wore a baseball cap to cover the hair loss he'd suffered as a result of chemotherapy, but he was otherwise the same wonderful Mike we'd known all along, funny, charming, upbeat, and totally certain that he was going to beat the leukemia. And so was everyone. There was no way that Mike Ockrent would lose his battle, for he was a tower of strength, a cool and indomitable leader, a man whom everyone looked up to with awe and admiration.

He was in and out of Sloan-Kettering several times during the rest of the year. Tragically Mike Ockrent died in early December 1999. Everyone was devastated, most especially Stro. Mike was the dearest love of her life, and while they'd known each other for eight years, they'd only been married for four and were still in a way almost honeymooners. She'd been so proud. She'd just directed her first show, *Contact,* which she'd also choreographed and conceived with author John Weidman, and it had opened in early fall to through-the-roof rave reviews. (*Contact* went on to win the Tony Award for the Best New Musical of the year 2000, along with a Tony for Stro herself, for choreography.) But the success of *Contact* was now nothing but a bitter irony—having a hit in the theater is meaningless when you've lost the one person most precious to you in all the world.

Soon after Mike died, Stro told us that we'd have to find somebody else to choreograph *The Producers,* since she might not be going back to work for a very long time and she didn't want us to delay our musical because of her. At this point, however, having seen her brilliant directorial work in *Contact,* we decided that we'd try to convince Stro not only to choreograph *The Producers* but also to direct it. We loved

Stro and believed it was critically important for her to throw herself body and soul into her work rather than sit alone in some dark room, grieving. In the sorrow-filled weeks following Mike's death, we browbeat, pestered, cajoled, and almost literally forced her to return to work on *The Producers.* At last, one bright late-winter day, she said yes, she'd do it. She plunged herself back into the theater at once and, for the next year and a half, set herself a grueling schedule of working twelve- and fourteen-hour days, seven days a week. Always bright, always smiling, always up, she confided to us later that she left her tears for when she got home late, alone, to the apartment she'd shared with Mike.

So our search for a director had ended. With Mike's spirit both in her heart and standing at her shoulder, Susan Stroman directed and choreographed *The Producers.* We could not have found, in all the world, a better person to do the job.

BAGEL MORNINGS AND TUNA FISH-AND-TOMATO-ON-RYE-TOAST AFTERNOONS

WINTER & SPRING, 2000 — TOM talks

Oh, my God, watch out! Mel is wielding a large and frighteningly sharp-looking carving knife. "Stand back and none of you will get hurt," he cries. It is shortly after 10:30 a.m. on a chill Tuesday morning in early February 2000, and what has recently become a thrice-weekly ritual is once again about to unfold in the spacious gourmet kitchen of Stro's West 57th Street apartment. Mel is standing at a carving board with the knife in hand as Stro, Glen, and I cautiously back away from him. He is ready now, the master bagel cutter, to slice the bagels that—once toasted by the master bagel toaster (who else, of course, but Mel?)—will be the centerpiece of the procrastination-to-keep-from-starting-to-work-on-our-script brunch of fresh orange juice, freshly made Zabar's coffee, and toasted bagels slathered with cream cheese.

Mel is struck with a great idea. "We'll sell 25,000 percent, take the money, and go to Rio."

Stro provides all of the fixings, including three different kinds of bagels, but it is Mel who always insists on preparing the bagels, while Stro makes the coffee, Glen pours the orange juice, and I idly contribute nothing but small talk while sitting impatiently at the kitchen table awaiting my brunch. Mel has taken on the role of the

father in the psychodrama of our little nuclear family, while Stro, although a full generation younger than both Mel and me, is the mother, Glen is the eagerly helpful son, and I'm the wastrel, drunken Irish uncle. In any event, Mel, revealing yet another of his myriad talents, has turned out to be a world-class slicer and toaster of bagels. Deftly, neatly, with the steady hand and awe-inspiring precision of a neurosurgeon, Mel slices each of the bagels into three exactly equal parts, two outer crusts and a crustless center section. And within minutes he has calmly sliced a dozen bagels in this impressive manner and is ready to begin his toasting. And soon, in the warm, cozy kitchen on a cold New York winter morning, all four of us are huddled happily together around the round kitchen table munching our perfectly toasted bagels. Our work session has been scheduled for three hours, from 10 a.m. until 1 p.m. Since Mel had as usual turned up somewhat late for the meeting and is in no rush as he prepares the bagels, it is now 11 a.m. and we've effectively killed one hour of our three-hour working session. Thus are landmark, smash-hit Broadway musicals created, and that's why they seem to take so long to get written.

The toasting of bagels. They are not, God forbid, to be even slightly burned, nor are they to be embarrassingly undercooked, but are instead to be toasted a light golden brown. And Mel, to give him his due, hovering over the toaster, cocking his ear to listen, sniffing, seems to have some kind of sixth sense when it comes to knowing when a bagel has been toasted to perfection and is ready to face the world. Instead of waiting for it to pop up by itself, he does it, at precisely the correct moment. Next, burning his fingers, he yanks the toasted bagel out of the toaster with a cry of "Yeow!"

Following brunch, we adjourn at last to Stro's living room and sit exactly where we always sit: Glen at the upright Steinway, Stro curled up in an easy chair near the piano, Mel relaxed in a second easy chair across the room, and I on the couch with our working script and a fresh yellow legal pad spread out in front of me on the coffee table. No more lollygagging; we are going to work. The first subject of the morning: whether or not the song "We Can Do It!" sung by Bialystock to Bloom in Act One, Scene 2, would be helped by an introductory verse. "We Can Do It!" is one of the earliest songs that Mel wrote for the show, way back in the summer of 1998, and it has never had a verse. But Glen has recently had the idea that it could use one, to make the song feel less blatant and on-the-nose, to be a kind of launching pad into an opening chorus that baldly begins, "We can do it, we can do it, we can do it, you and me!"

The previous afternoon, at Glen's apartment, Mel had turned out a seven-line draft of the verse that Glen and I thought was pretty damn good. Mel had quickly come up with a tune, too, that served nicely to house the verse, and Glen had carefully written out Mel's notes.

The basic idea, which Glen had come up with, was to cite great moments in history when somebody might have cried out "We can do it!" to somebody else. Within a few minutes, we'd come up with Lewis and Clark and the pair who'd first conquered Mount Everest, the English mountain climber Sir Edmund Hillary and his Sherpa guide, Tenzing. But we could think of few others and were uncertain about using "Hillary," which might sound as though we were going for some kind of Clinton joke. We next thought of Washington as he crossed the Delaware. But that would be almost impossible to put into a lyric, Glen and I agreed, because there was absolutely nothing that rhymed with Delaware. Glen and I continued thinking while Mel sat with his head back and his eyes closed, almost as though asleep, for three or four minutes. And then Mel opened his eyes. "You're going to like this," he said. "'Well aware.' 'Well aware' rhymes with Delaware." Soon he was dictating fragments of lines that I put down on my legal pad, adding and crossing out as he'd change his mind or have a second thought about a rhyme, and after we'd been working for perhaps four hours—with only a brief break for each of us to down a tuna fish on toasted rye, dry with no butter or mayonnaise, with a slice of tomato, no lettuce, ordered by phone and sent up from a nearby Korean deli—Mel had completed the seven-line verse that went like this:

What did Lewis say to Clark
When everything looked bleak?
What did Sir Edmund say to Tenzing
As they struggled toward Everest's peak?
What did Washington say to his troops
As they crossed the Delaware,
I'm sure you're well aware . . .

This is the verse we take up to Stro's apartment the next morning. Glen, who has worked closely with Stro as her dance-music arranger on a whole bunch of shows as well as on a ballet, has told us more than once, in awed seriousness, "Stro is *never* wrong." If she likes something, you keep it in, and if she doesn't like something, you damn well get rid of it fast because it's no good. And in recent months we've come to agree with him. She has an uncanny sense of what works and what doesn't work in a musical—it's something that, simply enough, you have to call genius.

Glen sits at the piano and plays and sings the verse for Stro. What does she think, yes or no? She smiles her great big beautiful smile. "Yes," she says. She likes it for exactly the reason that Glen had thought we needed it—because it gives the singer a platform from which he can powerfully launch himself into the opening chorus. It's bright, it's funny, and it works. Stro has a suggestion, however. After Max has sung "I'm sure you're well aware . . . " and is about to go into "We can do it!" how about having Leo interject a short line of dialogue? Like what? "Like," says Stro, "he could in his wide-eyed innocent way ask, 'What did they say?'" Yes, we all like that! It helps the verse, it helps the song.

The lesson in all this? Only that a musical is the sum of hundreds and hundreds, maybe even thousands of such fragments and that careful attention must be paid to all of them. You have to focus on each one for whatever length of time it takes to get it right. A musical really can't be dashed off but is instead the product of a group of pretty smart and very dedicated people who are willing to work endless hours together for weeks, months, and perhaps years to get the damn thing right.

Such total commitment will take you a long way toward creating a successful show, but to this diligence must also be added one crucial element—courage. Mel Brooks's greatest piece of advice to all those who've ever worked with him: "If you walk up to the bell, you've got to ring it!" In other words, no timid half-jokes, no nervous worrying about whether your work is going to offend somebody or other, but just do it, loud and clear, ring the bell that your heart and your brains tell you is the right bell to ring. The funniest lines, the truest moments, no matter what. Write them or don't write anything at all.

To backtrack a bit. From the early spring of 1999 and all the way to the end of the year, during the sad days of Mike's illness and his passing, Mel and I continued to work, often with Glen but more often alone, writing *The Producers* both in New York, getting together usually at his Upper East Side apartment, and in Los Angeles, in his Culver Studios office. By the time I was writing of our "bagel mornings and tuna fish–with–tomato–on–rye–toast afternoons," we'd pretty much gotten an entire draft of the book finished. And Mel had completed fairly advanced drafts of all the songs, too.

But then there was the show's opening number. Early on, I'd had an idea for the opening of the show that Mel thought was great. Rather than starting the musical where the movie had started, with the first meeting of Bialystock and Bloom in Bialystock's office, I suggested that it might start instead on a Broadway stage in the middle of the finale of Bialystock's latest flop musical. With such an opening, an all-singing, all-dancing parody of a fiasco, the audience would happily discover right away that the musical of *The Producers* was going to be its own thing and not simply a slavish copy of

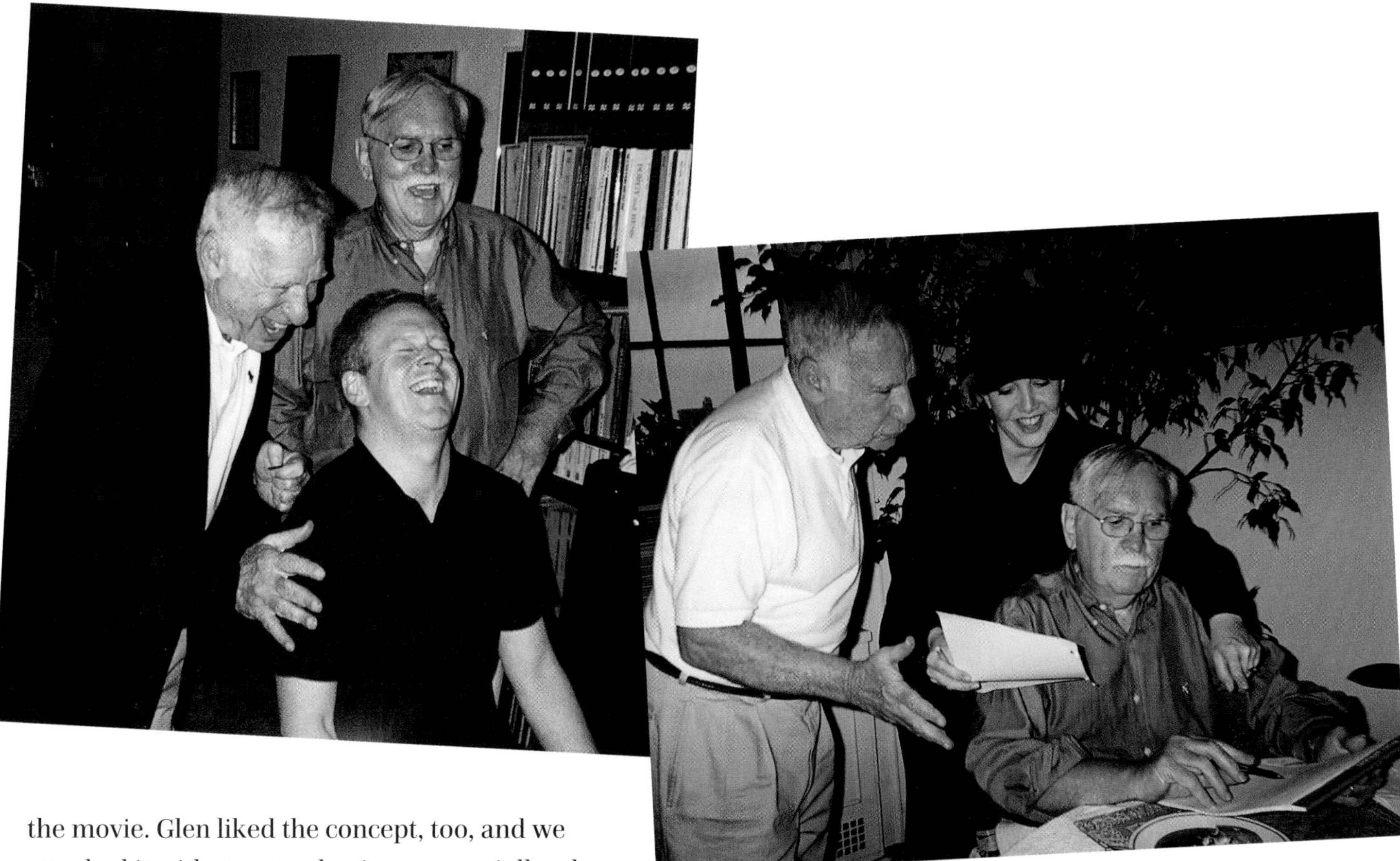

the movie. Glen liked the concept, too, and we attacked it with great enthusiasm, especially when Mel hit upon the idea of Bialystock's flop being a blatant rip-off of *Oklahoma!* entitled *Hey, Nebraska!* Mel, with Glen's help, quickly came up with a medley of tunes that sounded almost exactly like tunes from *Oklahoma!* but weren't; meanwhile Glen and I also had a hilarious time encouraging Mel to write marvelous parodies of Oscar Hammerstein: "Oh, the corn is as high as a homesteader's fly," etc., etc.

All three of us loved *Hey, Nebraska!* but when we played and sang it for others out in California, including Anne Bancroft and Alan Schwartz, they didn't like it. Too sophomoric, they said, too much like something from a Harvard Hasty Pudding show. And, they added, it would send an incorrect message to the audience—that the show was to be nothing more than a series of clever Mel Brooks parodies but not a genuine Broadway book musical. *Hey, Nebraska!* quickly went the way of "You'll Find Your Happiness in Rio"—into the nearest dumpster. "Okay," I said, "then what if we begin instead with the audience coming out of the theater following the opening night of Bialystock's latest flop and singing their reaction to the rotten show they've just seen?" Mel and Glen both eagerly jumped on the idea. They loved it. And within only a few days Mel had written a new song, "Opening Night," that seemed to be exactly right. It gleefully attacked both Bialystock's show, *Funny Boy,* a new musical version of *Hamlet,* and poor Bialystock himself.

ABOVE LEFT: *Glen turned out to be not only a sensational musician but also a walking encyclopedia of Hollywood and Broadway musicals. He knew all of Mel's credits, including the most obscure, like the fact that in 1957 he'd been the coauthor (with the late Joe Darion, who was later to write the eloquent lyrics of the great* Man of La Mancha*) of the book of a short-lived Broadway musical called* Shinbone Alley. *Even Mel had almost forgotten that.*

ABOVE: *Tom is confused. Mel has given him an old* Show of Shows *script. (Stro likes it!)*

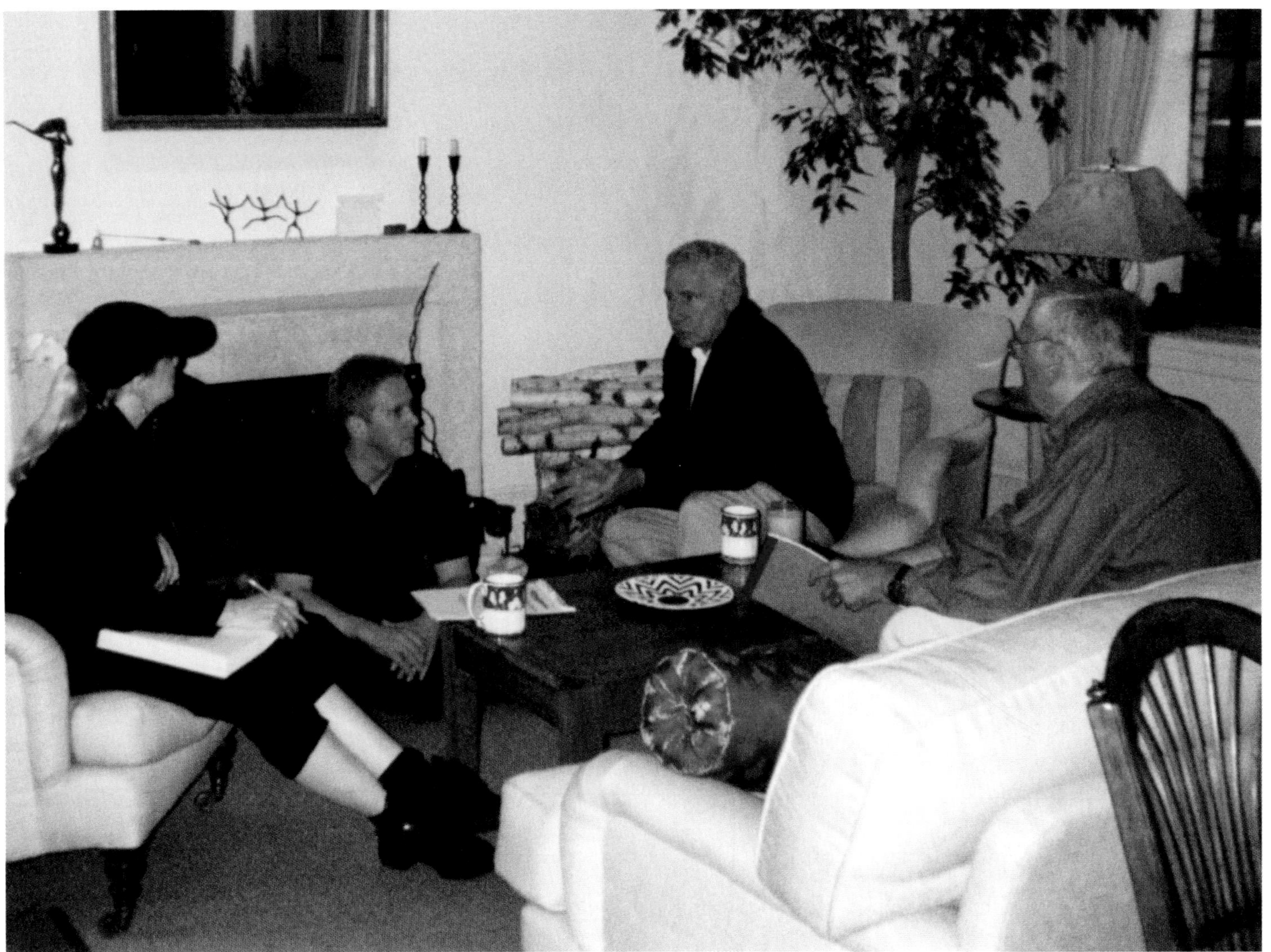

With what we agreed was a terrific opening for the show in hand, all of us—Mel, Stro, Glen, and I—decided that it was high time we got some feedback on what we'd written. We needed to find out if *The Producers* was any good at all. So Stro got in touch with Johnson-Liff, the brilliant New York casting agents who'd cast several of her previous shows, and asked them to put together a group of Broadway performers to do a reading of our script. The reading would be mainly for us, plus a crowd of our family and close friends, and also, of course, for our producer, David Geffen, the man who would be putting up the money, all by himself, to back the show. We begged Johnson-Liff to please get, if at all humanly possible, our first and only choice for the role of Max Bialystock, Nathan Lane, to star in the reading. And if you've been reading carefully, you already know that they succeeded in getting not only Nathan but also Gary Beach and Cady Huffman. The reading was set for Sunday, April 9, 2000, in New York.

On Tuesday, April 3, however, when Mel was just about to fly to New York for the reading but was still in Los Angeles, he got a call at his Culver Studios office that was to throw all of us into a state of chaos. The call was from David Geffen. He wasn't going to be coming east to attend our reading. In fact, because of the enormous pressures of his job at DreamWorks SKG, which were far greater than he'd imagined a couple of years earlier, he simply wasn't going to have the time to be the hands-on producer of a major Broadway musical. In short, while wishing us all the luck in the world, he was reluctantly forced to withdraw from the project. (We are all forever grateful to David for having gotten *The Producers* off the ground and for his determination to see Mel's movie turned into a hit Broadway musical.) For two years, we'd gone along cockily thinking that we'd never have to face the huge problem that faces every other musical hoping to go to Broadway—raising the money—because we already had Geffen backing us. But now we were both without a producer and without a dime of the $10 million we estimated the show would cost.

What to do? We considered canceling the Sunday reading, but then decided that we still needed to hear it read. A reading would tell us what worked and what didn't. The reading would go on. We had the actors, we had the room, we'd rented a piano; what we needed were producers. So we got on the phone to every producer, theater owner, and major theatrical investor that any of us chanced to know and invited them to the reading. It was embarrassingly late on Wednesday to invite Broadway's big shots to turn up for a Sunday reading. So what! We manned the phones and, among the four of us, managed to get together the crowd of fifty-odd producers who walked in the door, as recounted at the beginning of these pages.

Cady and Bryn Dowling, future chorine

THE AFTERMATH OF NERVOUS SUNDAY—A GO SHOW!

••••••

APRIL 10, 2000, AND BEYOND — MEL talks

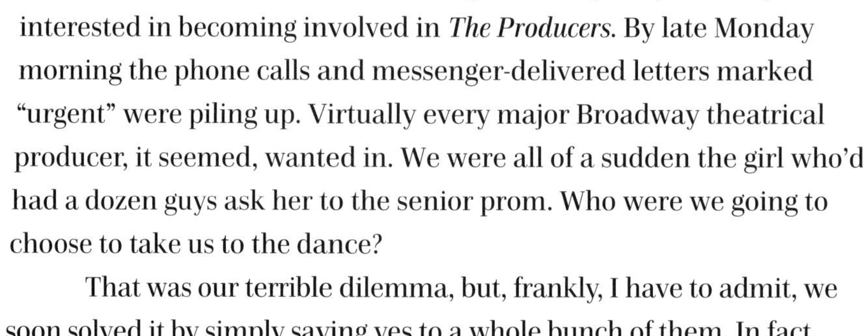

It was April 10, the Monday morning after the nervous Sunday afternoon and, oh, boy, were we in trouble. We were faced with a huge, brand-new problem. I'd asked the producers and investors who'd been at the reading to call my lawyer if they were interested in becoming involved in *The Producers.* By late Monday morning the phone calls and messenger-delivered letters marked "urgent" were piling up. Virtually every major Broadway theatrical producer, it seemed, wanted in. We were all of a sudden the girl who'd had a dozen guys ask her to the senior prom. Who were we going to choose to take us to the dance?

"Drink champagne 'til he pukes."

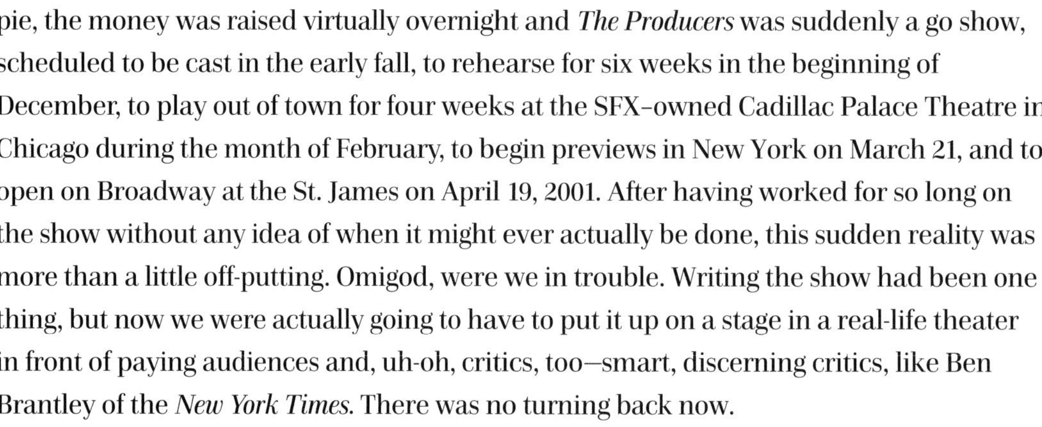

That was our terrible dilemma, but, frankly, I have to admit, we soon solved it by simply saying yes to a whole bunch of them. In fact, within a couple of weeks, we'd put together a consortium of no fewer than fourteen producers, led by Rocco Landesman, who gave us the St. James Theatre, as promised, and including Richard Frankel, who became both one of our producers and our general manager, along with SFX Theatrical Group (the owner of major theaters all over America); the founder and former owner of SFX Entertainment, Robert F. X. Sillerman, who sold SFX for a remarkable sum; and, believe it or not, even me! Anyway, with each of the fourteen producers taking only a slice of our $10 million investment pie, the money was raised virtually overnight and *The Producers* was suddenly a go show, scheduled to be cast in the early fall, to rehearse for six weeks in the beginning of December, to play out of town for four weeks at the SFX-owned Cadillac Palace Theatre in Chicago during the month of February, to begin previews in New York on March 21, and to open on Broadway at the St. James on April 19, 2001. After having worked for so long on the show without any idea of when it might ever actually be done, this sudden reality was more than a little off-putting. Omigod, were we in trouble. Writing the show had been one thing, but now we were actually going to have to put it up on a stage in a real-life theater in front of paying audiences and, uh-oh, critics, too—smart, discerning critics, like Ben Brantley of the *New York Times.* There was no turning back now.

Indeed, seriously large checks amounting to $10 million had been written. Contracts were being drawn up, negotiations were going on, money was coming in, and money was going out. Per our instructions, Nathan Lane was being hotly pursued to sign for the role of Max Bialystock, and so was our dream choice to play Leopold Bloom, the sensationally talented Matthew Broderick. Meanwhile, rafts of new people were swarming aboard. For a long time, basically four of us—Tom, Glen, Stro, and I—had been working on *The Producers*, but now all of a sudden it seemed as though there were nearly four hundred of us.

With our blessing and total agreement, Stro was putting together the show's design team, lining up a staggeringly talented group with whom she'd worked on previous shows and whom she also considered her friends: a trio of guys, Stro assured us, who were the best possible people to design *The Producers*, and the nicest and the easiest to work with as well. They were:

Scenery designer Robin Wagner: a member of the Theatre Hall of Fame and the winner of literally dozens of major theatrical awards, including several Tony and Drama Desk Awards. Taciturn, cool, a soft-spoken storyteller with a wonderfully dry wit, Robin had designed a pair of Stro's earlier shows, *Crazy for You* and *Big*.

Costume designer William Ivey Long: another winner of a shelfful of major theatrical awards, including a bunch of Tonys, Drama Desk Awards, etc., for shows like *Nine, Crazy for You, Guys and Dolls, Cabaret*, and *Chicago*. An amiable and immensely likable North Carolinian, he'd also done no fewer than six previous shows with Stro.

Lighting designer Peter Kaczorowski: once again, as distinguished as they come, a multiple award winner for his lighting of dozens of major Broadway and Off Broadway shows. Quietly reserved and meticulously hardworking, he had done the lighting design for both of Stro's current Broadway hits, *Contact* and *The Music Man*.

With this Broadway dream team assembled, it was definitely not the time for Tom, Glen, and me to pack our bags and head for the beach. Instead, we had to get to work immediately fixing all of the things that we'd realized were wrong with the show during the April 9 reading. First and foremost—especially since we so desperately wanted Nathan Lane to play Bialystock and had learned that he was somewhat on the fence about whether or not to do it—we knew we had to write a big show-stopping number for Nathan to perform alone late in the show's second act. Since he wasn't in "Springtime for Hitler," he had to have his own one-man equivalent, an eleven o'clock tour de force in the tradition of numbers like "Rose's Turn" in *Gypsy*.

So, once again, Tom and I began meeting daily, afternoons from one to five, with Glen in his apartment. First problem to solve: Where the hell can this eleven o'clock number take place? An idea quickly surfaced. At the end of the office scene following "Springtime for Hitler," Bialystock is arrested and taken off to jail, while Bloom and Ulla run off together to Rio. The next scene takes place in the downtown New York City

TOP: *Production stage manager Steve Zweigbaum*

CENTER: *Ira Mont—Brooklyn's own stage manager to the stars!*

BOTTOM: *Doug Besterman, boy orchestrator, soon to pick up his second Tony (for* The Producers*)*

Stro, Mel, Warren Carlyle, and Lisa Shriver. Warren Carlyle is a movie-star-handsome Englishman who'd done sterling work for Stro when she'd choreographed the celebrated 1999 London revival of Oklahoma! *Lisa is a slim and beautiful young blonde from Colorado, not only a hell of a dancer but also a wickedly funny wisecracker who is almost faster on the comic draw than Mel Brooks. Lisa and Warren were at Stro's side through the entire rehearsal period, the Chicago run, and our New York previews right up until opening night.*

courtroom where Bialystock is on trial and is surprised by the return of Bloom and Ulla from Rio. What if, we now thought, instead of moving immediately on to the courtroom scene, we wrote a new scene in which Bialystock is found alone in a jail cell, lamenting his fate? Good idea! It would move the book forward, slightly, and it was a logical place to find Bialystock isolated and in the kind of highly emotional state that would justify a big song. (A basic guideline in writing musicals: A character may burst into song only when the emotion he is feeling–be it love, hate, despair, or what have you–is too overwhelming to be expressed in mere spoken words but instead can only be sung.) We get a brainstorm. What if Bialystock, knowing that he's bound to be found guilty and spend the next several years in jail, disgraced and forever finished as a producer, sang a song of farewell to Broadway, a kind of old-fashioned, sentimental, George M. Cohan-type song laced with funny and ironic lyrics–"Goodbye to Broadway."

Not bad, we all thought, and maybe even pretty good. Who knew? We took "Goodbye to Broadway" to Stro for her reaction. And, remember, Stro is *never* wrong. Glen played and sang it. Okay, Stro, yes or no? She smiled her great big beautiful smile. "I'm sorry, guys, but no," said Stro, going on to explain that even as a kind of parody it was too sentimental, as well as not dynamic enough to blow the roof off the theater. Stro had strongly voted no, but we weren't yet quite ready to give up on the idea entirely. And so all four of us, including a somewhat reluctant Stro, agreed to have Glen perform it for Nathan Lane. Maybe he'll like it more than Stro, we thought; maybe he'll see the comic possibilities in it. But maybe he wouldn't. And he didn't. Nathan agreed entirely with Stro–the song, he felt, was too soft and definitely not a showstopper. So it was goodbye forever to "Goodbye to Broadway" and back to the old drawing board.

Back to Glen's apartment and back to each of us thinking out loud.

What was Bialystock feeling, alone in his cell? Angry, abandoned, *betrayed!* And what if we heightened these emotions by opening the scene in the jail cell with Max receiving a cheery postcard from Leo and Ulla describing what a great time they're having in Rio without him? This would drive him mad, furious, and launch him into a litany of rage at Leo. In a matter of only three days we'd written the song "Betrayed," a five-minute-long raving nervous breakdown of a number that gave Nathan full leeway to go screamingly over the top and stop the show. This time I felt that I'd gotten what we'd been looking for and, thank God, Stro heartily agreed and so did Nathan. In fact, I think that it was having the chance to do "Betrayed" that tipped the scales on Nathan's part to decide in favor of doing *The Producers.* I am proud, too, and not even a little bit humbled, to let it be known that "Betrayed" brings down the house and stops the show with waves of cheers and applause every single time that Nathan goes out there on stage and does it. I am forever grateful to Nathan for his sensational and already legendary performance of "Betrayed," and I am also forever grateful to Glen Kelly for his invaluable assistance in helping me to shape the number and make it work.

Rewrites and cutting would, of course, have to be done during rehearsals, during our out-of-town Chicago tryout, and during New York previews, but, for now, with the addition of "Betrayed" to the show, the writing of *The Producers* was at last, after over two years of work, complete. Now, as our designers were frantically designing away, we had to find the perfect cast to play all of our wonderfully demanding roles. Onward!

CASTING

AUTUMN 2000 — TOM talks

Hallelujah! Fabulous news! It's early October 2000, and after months of negotiating, both Nathan Lane *and* Matthew Broderick have agreed to be in *The Producers*! We've landed the perfect pair to play Bialystock and Bloom! Everything's coming up roses! We've also happily signed both Gary Beach (as Roger De Bris) and Cady Huffman (as Ulla), who were equally sensational in the April reading. We have only two principal roles left to cast–the wacko neo-Nazi playwright, Franz Liebkind, and Roger De Bris's "common-law assistant," Carmen Ghia.

In mid-October, as auditions for *The Producers* got under way, we saw dozens of applicants for the role of Liebkind and ultimately picked the immensely talented Ron Orbach. A big, jolly bear of a man, hardworking beyond belief and intensely determined, Ron was just starting to truly shine in the role of Liebkind when, during one of the final rehearsals in Chicago before our first Cadillac Palace performance, he blew out his left knee while executing a particularly difficult dance step. The diagnosis: Ron needed an immediate operation and had to step out of the show, to be replaced by his swing/understudy,

Mel is happy. He's found his bloom, his perfect Leo Bloom.

Brad Oscar. By the time Ron's knee had healed, his understudy had emerged as a huge favorite with audiences in Chicago, and, in consequence, we made the painful decision to turn the role over to Brad permanently. For Ron it was certainly the unhappiest story in the annals of *The Producers*, but for Brad it was nothing short of a miracle, and his performance earned him a Tony nomination.

Back during the auditions for Franz Liebkind, as I was sitting between Mel and Stro at the table where we were assessing the various applicants, an actor appeared that I'd seen in several shows and thought was terrific. "Watch this guy, Roger Bart," I whispered to Mel. "He's very good. He won the Tony for Best Featured Actor in a Musical last year, playing Snoopy in *You're a Good Man, Charlie Brown*."

Roger read the role of Liebkind, and, frankly, he was disappointing, not really right for the part. "What do you think?" I asked Mel.

"Uh-uh, no good, too short for Liebkind," said Mel. Stro nodded in agreement and dismissed Roger with a cheerful "Thank you." Roger thanked us in return and glumly exited.

"Wait a minute. I've got an idea," cried Stro, leaping up and running out of the room after Roger.

Matt Loehr as Sabu and Abe Sylvia as the very friendly Cherokee Indian

"She's wrong. The guy can't play Liebkind," said Mel with a shake of his head.

"Stro's wrong?" I said. "But you and I both know that Stro is never wrong."

In a few moments, Stro returned, and ten minutes later Roger Bart came back into the room with an entirely different set of lines Stro had asked him to read–the role of Carmen Ghia. Roger began, and instantly we all knew that we'd found our ideal "common-law assistant." Once again, Stro wasn't wrong, and with the casting of Roger Bart (Carmen Ghia to perfection) and Ron Orbach a day or two later, we'd found all six of our principals.

There are big musicals and little musicals, but every musical needs to have at least a couple of spectacular, eye-opening production numbers in which the stage is lavishly filled with a company of beautiful people. Musicals like the mid-1990s Broadway revival of *Show Boat*, for instance, featured numbers with as many as sixty-five singers and dancers on stage. Nonetheless, for both financial and artistic reasons, Stro had determined that *The Producers* should be lean and mean, with only twenty-two in its cast. The six principals plus six character people, three men and three women, along with a ten-member ensemble of singers and dancers, six women and four men. But how do you do a seemingly

"Nice work if you can get it." **BELOW, LEFT TO RIGHT:** *Christina Marie Norrup, Ida Gilliams, Kimberly Hester, Tom, Tracy Terstriep, Mel, Angie L. Schworer, Bryn Dowling, and Adrienne Gibbons*

Boys are girls in Little Old Lady Land, and girls are boys in the Hitler auditions.

huge number like "Springtime for Hitler" with so small a cast? If you are Susan Stroman, you figure out that everyone in the ensemble, as well as the six character people, can double and triple during the number, starting out as Bavarian peasants, for example, and returning moments later as tap-dancing Nazi storm troopers. And then, finally, they can make another amazingly quick backstage costume change and each come back on stage as an SS trooper ingeniously rigged up to a pair of dummies dressed as SS troopers, all marching downstage in lockstep in front of an enormous tilted mirror, creating the illusion that there are nearly a hundred performers on stage when, in fact, there are only eighteen. And in numbers in the show that call for a stageful of women, like our Act One finale, set in Little Old Lady Land and called "Along Came Bialy," all of our women played Little Old Ladies and so did half of our men. At the same time, in the Act Two Hitler audition scene, where the script called for a stageful of men, more than half of the Hitlers on stage were chorus girls dressed as men and wearing little slapped-on Hitler moustaches.

In September, Stro had held her auditions for the ensemble members and character people, with the aim of putting together a company of sensational dancers and terrific singers who could also handle small comic acting bits.

With Glen often playing piano for the auditions and our gifted musical director, vocal arranger, and orchestra conductor, Patrick S. Brady, now also on hand, Stro put the aspiring ensemble members, literally hundreds of them, through their paces with the help of her relentlessly cheerful and energetic dance department—Warren Carlyle, her associate choreographer and a talented full-fledged choreographer on his own, and Lisa Shriver, her assistant choreographer.

Stro has such a sterling reputation that all of New York's best dancers and singers always flock eagerly to her auditions. So *The Producers* had the pick of the litter, and Stro soon cast a sexy bevy of six gorgeous chorus girls. These "Broadway babes," as Stro liked to call them, could play Bloom's fantasized line of scantily clad chorines in "I Wanna Be a Producer," as well as the Ziegfeld-like showgirls who sinuously saunter down the staircase near the beginning of "Springtime for Hitler." The talented chosen six were Angie L. Schworer, Bryn Dowling, Kimberly Hester, Tracy Terstriep, Naomi Kakuk, and Ida Gilliams. Also cast were their two lovely and equally talented standbys (or swings), Adrienne Gibbons and Christina Marie Norrup. (Mel and I didn't contribute much to the dance auditions, other to wink and giggle at the lovely girls in their leotards—we were in chorus-girl heaven.)

Stro also had great good fortune in finding a wonderfully talented group of four singing and dancing ensemble men: Abe Sylvia, Matt Loehr, Robert H. Fowler, and Jeffry Denman—plus their swings, Brad Musgrove, Jamie LaVerdiere, and Brad Oscar.

Now we had only a half dozen other roles left, the character women and the character men who would be tapped to play the variety of relatively small comic acting roles. They also had to be top-drawer singers and dancers, so the right people were far from easy to find. Perhaps the toughest of these to cast was the little old lady, Hold Me–Touch Me, who dallies on the sofa with Bialystock. In the movie, the part had been played by one of the grand old ladies of the theater, Estelle Winwood, who'd been in her nineties when she'd done the part. But we couldn't hire a real little old lady, since the actress had to cover several parts, in addition to singing and dancing. So one afternoon after we'd seen dozens of unimpressive applicants, we were taken aback when a woman who looked to be in her late seventies or early eighties toddled into the room, bent over on a cane, and in a cracked, elderly voice asked for a chance to audition. Not wanting to be cruel, we agreed to let her read and then planned to show her politely out the door. She began. And, dammit, she was terrific, far better than any of the other actresses we'd heard. When she finished, we sighed and started to tell her, "Thank you, we're sorry, but . . ."

"But what?" she shouted, suddenly sounding years younger as she threw away her cane and whipped off her granny glasses and wig to reveal a vibrant and smiling young woman who was only in her thirties. Her name is Madeleine Doherty, and since our first public performance in Chicago, on February 1, 2001, she has had audiences in the palm of her gnarled hand as Hold Me–Touch Me.

Madeleine joined Jennifer Smith, who'd been a standout in the cast of our April 9 reading, and the ubiquitous Kathy Fitzgerald (probably best remembered by those who've seen *The Producers* as Shirley Markowitz, the very butch lighting director in "Keep It Gay") as our character women, and we also soon cast two brilliant character men, Peter Marinos and Ray Wills (who ended up playing no fewer than fourteen roles in the show), along with a character singer, Eric Gunhus. Eric, possessing the blond Aryan look of the quintessential Wehrmacht officer and the most glorious tenor voice we'd ever heard, was exactly the man we'd been searching for to step out on stage and sing those stirring lyrics first heard in the movie, "And now it's . . . springtime for Hitler and Germany./Deutschland is happy and gay!/We're marching to a faster pace./Look out, here comes the master race!"

The cast was cast. The die was cast, too, because like Bialystock and Bloom, we were in too deep to turn back.

As part of the audition, the ensemble candidates were asked to tell a joke. Here are the ones we could print:

Ray Wills: *A guy goes to the doctor. He has a carrot in each ear and two pickles up his nose. He says, "Doctor, what's wrong with me?" The doctor says, "Well, you're not eating right."*

••••••

Jennifer Smith: *Why do mice have little balls? Because they like to dance.*

••••••

Jeffry Denman: *I was in high school choir practice. We were in the midst of learning "Chim Chim Cheree," from* Mary Poppins. *Part of the lyrics are, "Or blow me a kiss, and that's lucky, too." The sopranos were not doing well and our choir director was getting upset. He then went one at a time down the row to see who knew the notes and who didn't. He did this very quickly. The first girl would sing, "Or blow me a kiss, and that's lucky, too." Good, next girl. "Or blow me a kiss . . . ," etc., etc. You had to be on his rhythm and ready when he got to you. Otherwise he'd yell at you. And he could yell. He made football players cry. One of the girls was so nervous and scared she was on the verge of tears. He finally got to her, and she clammed up completely. He got madder and madder. Finally he screamed at her, "Sing 'or blow me'! Sing 'or blow me'!"*

REHEARSALS, DAY 1 – BEDLAM!

•••••••

DECEMBER 11, 2000 — TOM talks

How many people are working on this damn show? On the sixth floor of the New 42nd Street Studios, in Studio A, an enormous throng is milling about at 11 a.m. on December 11, when *The Producers* is scheduled to begin its first day of five weeks of New York rehearsals. Not only is the entire cast on hand–twenty-two of them, plus five swings–meeting each other all together for the first time, but there is also our crew of stage managers, led by our witty, cool-headed veteran production stage manager/associate director, Steven Zweigbaum, who has previously stage-managed several of Stro's shows. The stage managers, along with a quartet of production assistants, add up to eight additional bodies, so that, with the cast, there are thirty-six people in the room. Plus our four-man music department, Glen Kelly, Patrick Brady, rehearsal drummer Cubby O'Brien (years ago, as a child actor, one of early TV's famed Mouseketeers), and rehearsal pianist Phil Reno. That makes forty. There are also Mel Brooks, me, Susan Stroman, and Stro's little dance department, Warren Carlyle and Lisa Shriver. Forty-five. And we're just getting started. Because, believe it or not, also in the room are:

- All of our designers–Robin Wagner, William Ivey Long, and Peter Kaczorowski, as well as our sound designer, Steve C. Kennedy, and our wig and hair designer, Paul Huntley–and their head assistants.
- Nancy Coyne and her staff of aides from Serino Coyne, Inc., our brilliantly creative ad agency.
- The entire staff of our public relations firm, Barlow-Hartman, run by John Barlow and Michael Hartman, a pair of coolly with-it young men-about-town (assisted by their tall and incredibly fabulous chief lieutenant, Bill Coyle).
- The members of our prop department, led by one of the nicest, brightest, and most hardworking women in all of show business, Laura Koch, and her chief assistant, James Cariot.

CLOSING NIGHT

- All fourteen of our producers and their chief aides, plus several of our associate producers. (An associate producer is someone who is willing to associate with a producer.) The fourteen producers were, and still are, Rocco Landesman, Rick Steiner, Richard Frankel, Tom Viertel, Robert F. X. Sillerman, Steven Baruch, Marc Routh, Bob and Harvey Weinstein (of Miramax Films), SFX Entertainment (led by Scott Zeiger and Miles Wilkin), James D. Stern, Douglas L. Meyer, and, lest we forget, Mel Brooks.
- Our company manager, Kathy Lowe, and our associate company manager, Jackie Newman.
- Our general manager, the fabulous Laura Green, delegated by her boss, Richard Frankel, our nominal general manager, to be our day-to-day, nuts-and-bolts general manager.
- Our orchestrator, the amiable, soft-spoken, and boyish-looking Tony Award winner (for *Fosse*), Doug Besterman.
- Our music coordinator (the man who hires the members of the orchestra), John Miller.
- At least a dozen photographers, madly shooting away in every direction for who knew what publications.

During rehearsals, Matthew kept Nathan floating on a sea of laughter.

- Mike Wallace and a film crew from *60 Minutes,* who, everyone is thrilled to hear, are preparing a segment on Mel Brooks and his musical to be aired on CBS on Sunday evening, April 15, four days before our New York opening.

So, all in all, I estimate, there are easily three hundred people in the room, most of them working on the show. And with so many bodies crammed in one room, a kind of larger-scale Marx Brothers stateroom scene, it is–to quote Roger De Bris in *The Producers*, going ballistic in the Hitler audition scene–"Bedlam, bedlam!"

This no ordinary rehearsal, of course, but instead a so-called meet-and-greet session. For the first and, in fact, the last time, everyone involved in putting together the show is assembled to introduce themselves and report on the progress of their various departments

Later, in the afternoon, after everyone but the cast and crew has left, there will be a first reading of the script, which goes extraordinarily well, especially when Nathan Lane electrifies everyone with his first-ever-anywhere performance of "Betrayed." There is also nonstop hilarious laughter from the cast throughout the reading. ("Meaningless," I tell Mel. "One of the cardinal rules of the theater is that you can never trust the reactions of cast members. We won't know if any of our lines are really funny until we've done the show for a real, live, paying audience.")

Earlier, by the way, during the bedlam, Mel and I had looked at one another with nostalgic sighs for what was now clearly a lost past. Whatever happened, we both wondered, to that cozy little family of four, so recently the sum total of everyone working on *The Producers*, huddled over their toasted bagels? Mel had told Stro that those days when the four of us were working together on the show were among the happiest in his whole life. And they'd been among the happiest in mine, too. But now they were obviously gone for good. The creating of *The Producers* had slipped out of our hands into the hands of hundreds of others. Although we'd be giving notes and doing rewrites in the back room during every rehearsal, it was no longer our show.

THE VERY WINDY CITY

LATE JANUARY & EARLY FEBRUARY 2001 — MEL talks

Welcome to the dead of winter in Chicago! It was the best of times, it was the worst of times. It was freezing cold, but there was a warm glow emanating from the Cadillac Palace Theatre, where all of us working on *The Producers*, far from home in a distant city, were snuggled together like newborn pups in a cardboard box.

Tom and Carolyn Meehan chill but still smiling in Chicago.

We saw each other day and night, from early-morning get-togethers for breakfast in hotel coffee shops to "ten out of twelve" noon-to-midnight technical rehearsals in the theater, and then on to late-night impromptu pizza-and-Cosmopolitan parties in our hotel's lounge, with Glen Kelly at the piano playing medleys of tunes by Kern, Gershwin, Porter, Berlin, and the ever-popular Mel Brooks.

Hard-nosed theatrical producers, looking only at the bottom line, invariably argue that it's a huge waste of money to take a show out of town. "You can do your trying-out in New York," they grumble, "and not lose a fortune schlepping an entire company of actors and twelve truckloads of scenery to some foreign city like Chicago." What they don't realize is that money spent on going out of town is not lost money but is instead wisely invested money. Because, first of all, when a show goes out of town, the actors get a chance to play for

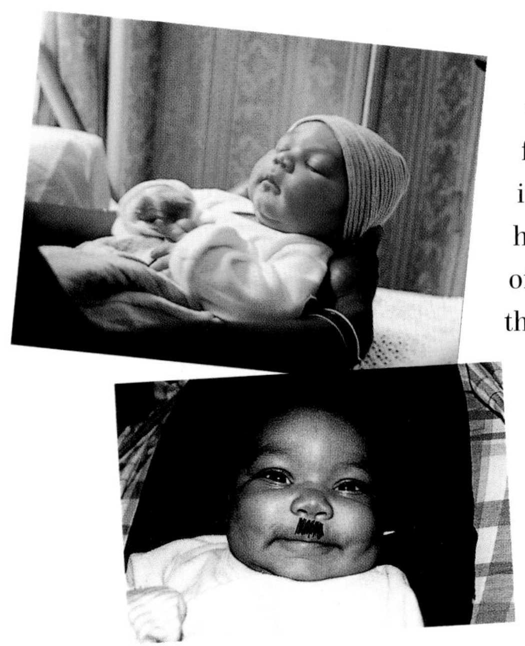

The last thing I said to my very pregnant girlfriend Shalyi as I boarded the plane to Chicago was, "Please, whatever you do, avoid going into labor February 1st. Squeeze, hang upside down, but keep that baby in." I was teasing, of course, but our first preview of The Producers *was scheduled for February 1, and I desperately wanted to be there. There was no question, however, that I wouldn't miss the arrival of my second child, also scheduled to debut February 1.*

And there were, in fact, twin debuts. The morning of February 1 I flew in a panic to New York, arriving in time for Eller's spectacular entrance. That afternoon I returned to Chicago, arriving just in time for the first spectacular preview.

*I figured I would most likely tank in the show that night or drop a line, miss an entrance, scenery would fall on me—*something *would happen because days like this just can't be that perfect. This one was.*

—Roger Bart
(Carmen Ghia)

audiences of non–New Yorkers who will be patient and not boo or walk out while a show is breaking in, giving the cast, especially of a comedy, a chance to fine-tune their performances in front of sympathetic crowds. And, equally important, going out of town gives everybody working on a show—away from home, family, and friends—an opportunity to bond, to become a happy bunch of pals all pulling together for the same goal: a great big fat smash hit. In fact, they even kind of grow to love one another. And, believe it or not, all that love makes its way across the footlights to the audience. That alone was worth the $2 million that our producers had complained they'd lose by going to Chicago. (In fact, the show didn't lose a cent in Chicago but actually made a little money, because the entire four-week run at the Cadillac Palace was quickly sold out.)

January 31, and there is a lot of anxiety on the part of the creators of the show, because for the first time tonight an audience will be in the theater, to attend our final dress rehearsal, which will be done with sets, costumes, and full orchestra. This is it, a real-life audience, albeit a nonpaying audience of invited friends of our Chicago-based producers who'll fill only half of the vast theater's 2,300 seats. Actually, Tom and I have been in an increasing state of anxiety ever since we hit Chicago, two weeks ago. In fact, since anxiety has a way of semi-paralyzing all peristaltic functions, bagels are now out and bran muffins are in. We're both staying at the Renaissance Hotel, four blocks from the theater, a distance we walk back and forth at least twice a day, scurrying side by side through the icy, wind-swept streets of Chicago, dressed in matching, bulky, black, ankle-length Land's End parkas with big hoods—I'd bought two and given one to Tom, who, being a classic absent-minded-professor type, would otherwise probably have forgotten to wear any coat at all. We were Tweedledum and Tweedledee, two very nervous guys.

Despite our nervousness, we'd had some exhilarating moments during our time in Chicago. Like our first sight of Robin Wagner's brilliant Shubert Alley set for the show's opening scene. Not to mention all the rest of his sets. We'd visited his workshop at 890 Broadway in New York a number of times to squint at little drawings and small models of the sets, but they hadn't meant much to us. However, to see Robin's stunning full-sized sets, gorgeously lighted by Peter Kaczorowski, was thrilling beyond belief. We'd had only words on paper, but now we had fully lit, three-dimensional sets, as well as William Ivey Long's inspired costumes and one knockout Susan Stroman dance number after another. Vagrant daydreams of turning the movie of *The Producers* into a Broadway musical comedy had come to life.

And now, too, my music was no longer being played only by Glen Kelly on a piano but instead by a full orchestra. The afternoon of Sunday, February 28, had been the most exciting and emotional time I'd had in Chicago, when the orchestra had assembled in the lower lobby of the Cadillac Palace for the so-called *Sitzprobe* (a German expression meaning to sit and proofread the notes of a musical score) and I'd heard my tunes played for the first time as brilliantly orchestrated by Doug Besterman (with a nice assist from Larry Blank). I'd been moved beyond imagining, sometimes almost to tears, especially at the orchestrations of my ballads, "That Face" and "'Til Him." I'd heard sounds in my own music that I'd never heard before, woodwinds led by flutes and reeds, French horns playing Doug's beautiful orchestrations. From the tips of my toes to the roots of my hair, I knew at last what it felt like to be a full-fledged Broadway-musical composer.

ABOVE: *Sitzprobe*

BELOW: *Gary Beach*

The January 31 dress rehearsal. There are eight hundred or so people in the theater, and from the moment the curtain rises, they go crazy for the show, laughing their heads off and cheering, and at the final curtain there is an instant standing ovation. After the first giddy flush of joy, Tom and I exchange worried glances. "Meaningless. This audience means nothing," says Tom, "because they're all friends, and what's more, they got in free. They don't count." "You're right," I said. "We're living in a fool's paradise if we think we have some kind of hit just because this audience loved it."

The following evening, February 1, we held our first public preview, before a full house of 2,300 *paying* customers. "Now we'll finally get a true indication of whether the show is any good or not," says Tom, "because at last we've got an audience that has no ax to grind, who aren't our friends, and who have paid to get in. This is it!" "Good," I say. "This is it. At last, a true indication." The audience goes even crazier for the show than the audience had the night before. They almost literally fall out of their seats laughing. Tom and I stand at the back of the theater at the end of the show, watching the ecstatic audience members filing out, all grinning from ear to ear. "Meaningless. This audience means nothing," says Tom. "A bunch of easy-to-please hog butchers to the world! They are absolutely no gauge of how a New York audience will react to the show." "You're right," I say. "We're living in a fool's paradise if we think we have some kind of hit just because this audience loved it."

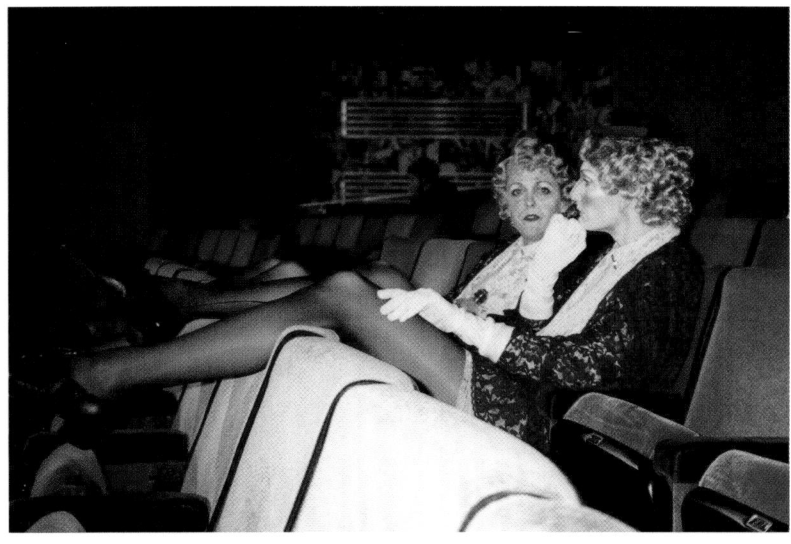

ABOVE: *Leggy little old ladies taking a break*

OPPOSITE: *Lisa Shriver kisses Nathan across the street.*

We desperately go on trying not to live in a fool's paradise for the next twenty laugh-filled previews. "We're never going to learn anything from these Chicago pushovers," says Tom. "But we can get some helpful input from the critics, especially from Richard Christiansen of the *Tribune*, the dean of the Chicago theater critics. He's always tough but fair; he'll give us some hard-edged insight into all of the many things that are wrong with the show." "Hard-edged insight. Good, that's what we're looking for," I say.

Chicago opening night, Sunday, February 18. The performance, before a gala audience of local notables, is a complete sensation. What do they know? We'll find out the real story in tomorrow's papers. Early the next morning, Tom and I anxiously pick up copies of the *Tribune* and, steeling ourselves for the worst, read Richard Christiansen's review. It opens with the following sentence: "Endless in its invention, relentless in its energy, extravagant in its design, witty in its silliness and shameless in its show bizziness, the stage musical of *The Producers* is an absolutely socko monster hit."

"What does he know?" Tom says, as I chime in with, "Oh, boy, are we in trouble." The New York critics, we agree, especially Brantley of the *Times*, will really be out for our scalps now. No out-of-town critic is going to dictate to them whether a show is a hit or not. After reviews like Christiansen's—and I'm afraid that we got several others almost equally ecstatic—we knew that we were bound to get slaughtered in New York. Time to blow town and say goodbye to the Windy City. How could Chicago have done this to us?

THE
the new
MEL BROOKS
musical

OPENING NIGHT

APRIL 19, 2001 — TOM talks

The long-awaited date, April 19, has at last come around, and at 6:30 p.m., an early curtain, the excited-out-of-their-minds cast will go out on the stage of the St. James Theatre to give the opening-night performance of *The Producers* before a packed house of family and friends, as well as a smattering of celebrities. I'm not in the least nervous. It's just that my hands are shaking so much that I can't get the studs into the front of my formal shirt so that I can get into my tuxedo and up to the theater in time for the curtain. My wife, Carolyn, steps in to do them for me. "Calm down, honey," she says. "I am calm!" I scream.

Matthew Broderick and Sarah Jessica Parker

All day long, in our downtown apartment on Jane Street, the phones have been ringing every minute with calls from well-meaning friends and family all over the country wishing me good luck. "Oh, my God, don't you know?" I've told them. "It's one of the oldest traditions of the theater, as well as part of a song in *The Producers*–It's bad luck to say 'good luck' on opening night." Now we're bound to get nothing but terrible reviews, especially from Ben Brantley in the *New York Times*. As I'd told Mel over and over again, a show can get lots of good reviews from other critics, but it can never be a genuine hit–our dream for *The Producers*–without getting a strongly favorable review from the critic of the *Times*. And, we somehow both sense, Brantley isn't going to go for our show. But we keep our fingers crossed, and I frankly couldn't be more excited.

After all, how many days in your life do you have your own brand-new $10 million musical opening on Broadway?

Buzz! The word had traveled from Chicago to New York with the speed of light (186,000 miles per second) that *The Producers* had the makings of a huge Broadway hit. And on March 21, when we began a month of New York previews at the St. James, the buzz was so strong that all 1,706 seats in the theater were totally sold out for every last one of the previews. Sitting in the back row on the side of the orchestra during the first of the New York previews, Mel and I were immensely relieved to discover that the hard-hearted audience of New Yorkers went just as wild for the show as had the soft-hearted audiences in Chicago.

"Maybe we've got ourselves a hit," said Mel. "Uh-uh, let's not get over-confident," I said. "Early preview audiences are made up of a whole lot of Broadway insiders, and *The Producers* is a show about their world, inside Broadway, so they're bound to love it because what we've written is a valentine to Broadway, an affectionate love letter to the whole business that also kids the pants off it." "So we don't have a real hit yet?" asked Mel. "No," I said. "We don't."

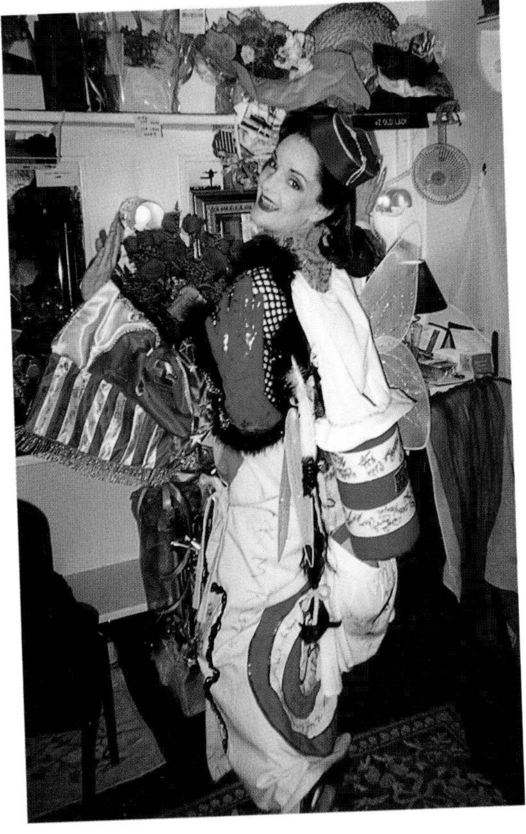

On our opening night, I received the Gypsy Robe from an ensemble member of the last Broadway musical to open before The Producers. *In musical theater, a gypsy is a dancer/singer who moves quickly from show to show, hence the name Gypsy Robe. The tradition began as a gag on the opening night of* Call Me Madame *in 1950 and remains an opening night blessing to this day. The gypsy with the greatest number of Broadway credits receives the robe and runs around the circle of company members three times, making sure to touch every person's hand, to ensure the best of luck for opening night. I will eventually attach some bit of memorabilia from* The Producers, *with everyone's signature, to the robe. As a robe becomes laden with mementos, it is retired and a new plain muslin robe is initiated with feathers, paint, and souvenirs. Three of the retirees are in the permanent collection of the Smithsonian Institution.*

—Jennifer Smith
(ensemble member)

From the beginning of previews in Chicago, Mel, Stro, and I had all strongly felt that the biggest problem with the show was its length. Admittedly, the audiences loved it, but we were convinced that they would love it even more if it were shorter and sweeter. In Chicago, on Monday, February 19, a day off for the cast and the same day that Richard Christiansen's incredible rave had appeared, Mel, Stro, and I met with Glen Kelly and went through the script from beginning to end, line by line, making cut after cut during a seven-hour working session that reduced the running time of the show by some ten minutes. The next day, when we went to rehearsal and dictated the dozens of cuts to the members of the cast, who were jubilant over our spectacular reviews, they could scarcely believe

Baby blue blankets saluting Leo's ever-present baby blue blanket from the cast to Stro, Mel, and Tom on opening night

So it's the week before Thanksgiving 2000 and I'm in Branson, Missouri, playing Santa Claus in the Radio City Christmas spectacular.

My agent calls. "I think you should fly in for an audition on your day off next Monday. They're still looking for a standby for Nathan Lane," he says, and I'm making travel arrangements faster than you can say Bialystock and Bloom.

I get the job as the "swing guy." I'm now covering Max, Franz, Roger De Bris, and several men in the ensemble. These first weeks are overwhelming as I wonder how I'll learn all that material. But we swings have the utmost confidence in ourselves, dubbing ourselves the "super swings," able to take on any role and protect the freedom of all the actors.

Well, as fate would have it, I am the first super swing to have his powers tested. It's six days before previews begin in Chicago, and the actor playing Franz suddenly needs orthoscopic knee surgery. I'm on.

I knew things were going well, and Mel and Susan were very supportive and complimentary. I kept telling myself to enjoy every moment because soon I'd be back to learning all those other roles. Indeed, the original actor did come back and do several shows at the end of our Chicago run.

We arrive back in New York and I have a message from my agent. "Hello, Franz," he said. The producers and Tom and Mel wanted me to take over the role. I had hoped, I had dreamed, but I hadn't let myself really go there. Now I had my first principal role in what was clearly going to be a hit.

My amazing, wild ride continued. We recorded the album, opened to the most unanimous praise in recent history, and then broke records for Tony nominations and wins. I told myself I wasn't going to be nominated. When my name, the fifth and final name in the category, was announced, I truly felt that fantasy and reality had converged. At last, I understood exactly what "It's an honor to be nominated" means.

I sometimes can't believe this is my life. Let's face it, a kid couldn't ask Santa for a better present.

—Brad Oscar
(Franz Liebkind)

what they were hearing. "For Christ's sake," said Nathan, "what would you guys have done if we'd gotten bad reviews?"

But all through the rest of the Chicago run and the early New York previews we continued to cut and tighten the show, ultimately taking out another ten minutes so that the show the Chicago critics had so thrillingly raved about was twenty minutes shorter when it was seen by the New York critics. In musical comedy, a form that calls for fast-paced, nonstop fun and never wearing out your welcome by giving the audience too much of a good thing, less is always definitely more.

Just as we'd gotten the show down to a perfect running time, Glen locked himself away in his apartment and, taking all of Mel's tunes from the show, created a breathtaking, three-and-a-half-minute overture that we all loved. Nonetheless, we had to agree with Stro, who is never wrong, that Glen's overture made the show three and a half minutes too long. So, after being in for a couple of shows, it was cut. Mel and I insisted, however, that it was too good to be thrown away; it had to be preserved somewhere, somehow. Glen suggested putting it on the show's cast album, and there it can now be heard, taking its place beside the great overtures of shows like *Gypsy* and *Guys and Dolls.*

Now, however, there were no more cuts to be made, no more lines to be changed, and nothing left to write but thank-you notes—the show, as we say in the biz, was frozen. And it is opening night. I in my tuxedo, Carolyn resplendent in a gorgeous new Bergdorf-Goodman *schmatta,* sitting in the eighth row on the aisle not far from Mel, in his tuxedo, and Anne also resplendent in a gorgeous new Armani, all four of us biting our nails and waiting for the curtain to rise. And rise it soon does, on what is maybe the most terrific performance of *The Producers* that Nathan, Matthew, and the rest of the greatest cast on earth have ever given. The super-friendly audience, which includes all of our many investors, roars with laughter from the first joke onward and leaps to its feet at the end in a tumultuous standing ovation, giving the cast curtain call after

PASSAIC

curtain call. Even Mel and I, along with Stro, get summoned up on stage to take a bow and stand there, blinded by the flashing of a thousand cameras, grinning like fools and insanely happy.

But this is no time to be happy. The hour of decision is all but upon us. The New York reviews, including Brantley's review in the *Times*, will be on the streets in only a few hours. We adjourn uptown to Roseland, on West 52nd Street, for the show's opening-night party, to which a select crowd of a mere 1,700 guests has been invited, and over champagne and limp shrimp we sweat out the hours until the reviews appear. The party is, to say the least, a mob scene, cameras once again flashing, a band loudly playing show tunes, everyone pushing and shoving to elbow through the huge throng to the buffet tables. "Bedlam, bedlam!" It reminds me somewhat of the JFK election-night party I'd gone to in 1960. And the early returns are good.

Shortly after 11 p.m., word begins to spread rapidly around the room that all of the TV reviews are, without exception, over-the-top raves. So far, so okay.

A couple of hours and a couple of glasses of champagne later, the early editions of two of the morning newspapers, the *Daily News* and the *Post* turn up, and the review in each of them is sensational. "No new musical in ages has offered so much imagination, so much sheer pleasure," says the *Daily News*, adding, "It's wilder and wackier than the film!" And the *Post* says, "Everything terrific you've heard is 100% true! It's a cast-iron, super-duper mammoth old-time Broadway hit!"

"Congratulations," says everyone, coming up to me to shake my hand. "Congratulations, congratulations, you've got a hit!" "No, no," I protest. "Don't jinx us! We're not a hit until the *New York Times* says we're a hit. We're living in a fool's paradise if we think that just because . . . "

"Quiet, please! Everybody please be quiet!" Harvey Weinstein is at the microphone on the bandstand with Ben Brantley's *New York Times* review, which he'd like to read aloud to everybody. "Quiet please! Everybody please be quiet!"

Harvey reads the review. "How do you single out highlights in a bonfire?" Ben Brantley's review begins. "Everybody who sees *The Producers*–and that should be as close to *everybody* as the St. James Theatre allows–is going to be hard-pressed to choose one favorite bit from the sublimely ridiculous spectacle that opened last night. . . . It is, to put it simply, the real thing: a big Broadway book musical that is so ecstatically drunk on its own powers that it leaves you delirious, too." He ends up by calling the show "fast, fierce, shameless, vulgar and altogether blissful."

I take a deep breath. I think I'm almost about to cry. Ben Brantley, in the *New York Times*, loves *The Producers.* A whole lot. I make my way through a thrilled and cheering crowd over to Mel.

"All right," I say to him, "I give up. It's a hit."

"You're right, Tom," Mel says. "It's a hit." We shake hands and smile at each other with great big broad smiles. We are the happiest two Jews in town. Sorry, make that one Jew and one Irishman.

•••••••

THE END

Shubert Alley–Opening Night

Max Bialystock's Office, June 16, 1959

A New York Courtroom

SETS

The Rooftop of a Greenwich Village Apartment Building

How do you live up to the movie has always been the question on this show. The only possibility seemed to be to try to pay a kind of homage to all the excessive moments, the maddest highlights of all the musicals we'd ever seen. Starting with the kitschiest drop and some of the corniest ideas and little but the love of musical comedy to go on, it seemed logical to include moments from the *Ziegfeld Follies*, Radio City Music Hall, and *A Chorus Line*, but with a certain kind of comment. Perhaps it was the inspired insanity of Mr. Brooks or the truly adventurous leadership of our director that allowed us to do anything we could think of. But it was also the very large stage in Chicago that invited us to the edge of possibilities. When everything was in place we realized the one thing we had forgotten was the kitchen sink. But upon viewing the finished number we saw that it would have been a redundancy.

When we brought the show to the intimate St. James Theatre in New York, we began coping with a very different problem—how to make the show smaller. We ended up storing Act Two in the sides of the fly chamber in Act One, and at intermission, we let Act Two in and Act One fly out. Needless to say, this put pressure on the intermission transition, which had ballooned from the traditional fifteen minutes in Chicago to a bloated thirty-five minutes in New York! Each piece of scenery was coordinated and choreographed just as it might have been on stage. Finally, the backstage choreography got tighter and more practiced. Eventually, we got down to an acceptable interval. I can assure you the backstage workers on this show are not playing cards in the basement . . . or not at intermission, anyway.

—Robin Wagner

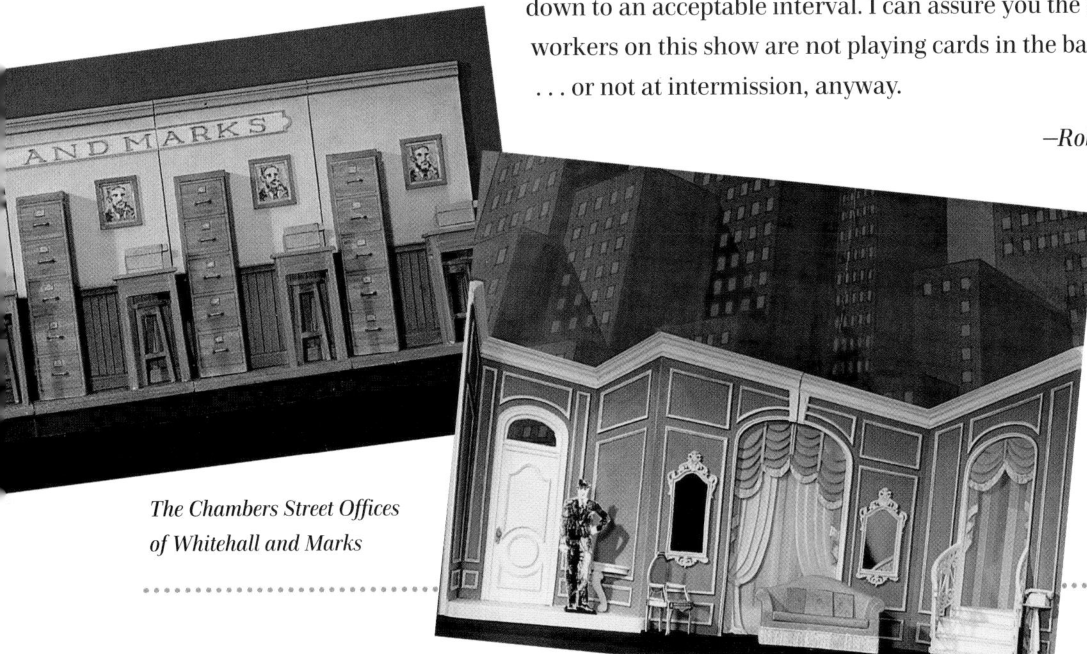

The Chambers Street Offices of Whitehall and Marks

The Living Room of Renowned Theatrical Director Roger De Bris's Elegant Eastside Townhouse

COSTUMES

Costumes for *The Producers* span continents (from New York City to Bavaria) and sensibilities (from Broadway usherettes to Nazi bratwurst showgirls). But the most challenging costume was the gown to be worn by Gary Beach as Roger De Bris. This needed to have a one, two, then three punch. As Roger descends the staircase in his "beautiful Upper East Side townhouse" dressed for the Choreographer's Ball, he must garner "ooohs" from the audience—for this is a *man in a dress* (first punch). Arriving downstage center, he announces to Max that he is dressed as the Grand Duchess Anastasia—and then he must look regal and Russian (second punch). Then he bemoans the fact that he fears he looks instead like the Chrysler Building—and he does—the silver Art Deco triangles on the front of his gown, formerly reading to the audience as elegant gown, then Russian court, now must instantly register as, of course, the *Chrysler Building* (third punch).

It was this one-two-three awareness game that had me stumped. During the out-of-town tryouts in Chicago, I landed the elegant gown, then the Russian court silhouette. But I missed the Chrysler image. I asked Susan and Mel if I could have another go at it. Back in New York, I draped brown paper on a dress form in the shape of a gown and attacked it with a magic marker, freehand. We then transferred my scratchings onto black net fabric; Bessie Nelson beaded it with bugle beads and jewels all by hand while watching television; and—voilà!—the one-two-three punch was achieved!

—*William Ivey Long*

LEFT: *Some of the 497 fabulous costumes designed by William Ivey Long*

ABOVE: *The versatile Kathy Fitzgerald plays ten different characters, running the gamut from bag lady to under-the-top chorus girl; she brings down the house as Roger De Bris's very butch lighting director.*

OPPOSITE: *The man of fourteen faces: Ray Wills just may break the record for number of costume changes in one show.*

Winner of 12

It's the night of the Tonys, June 3, and we're still the two happiest guys in town. **The Producers** *hadn't turned out to be a hit after all. It had turned out to be a smash hit, a mega-hit—the winner of more Tony Awards (twelve) than any show ever, two more than the ten that* Hello,

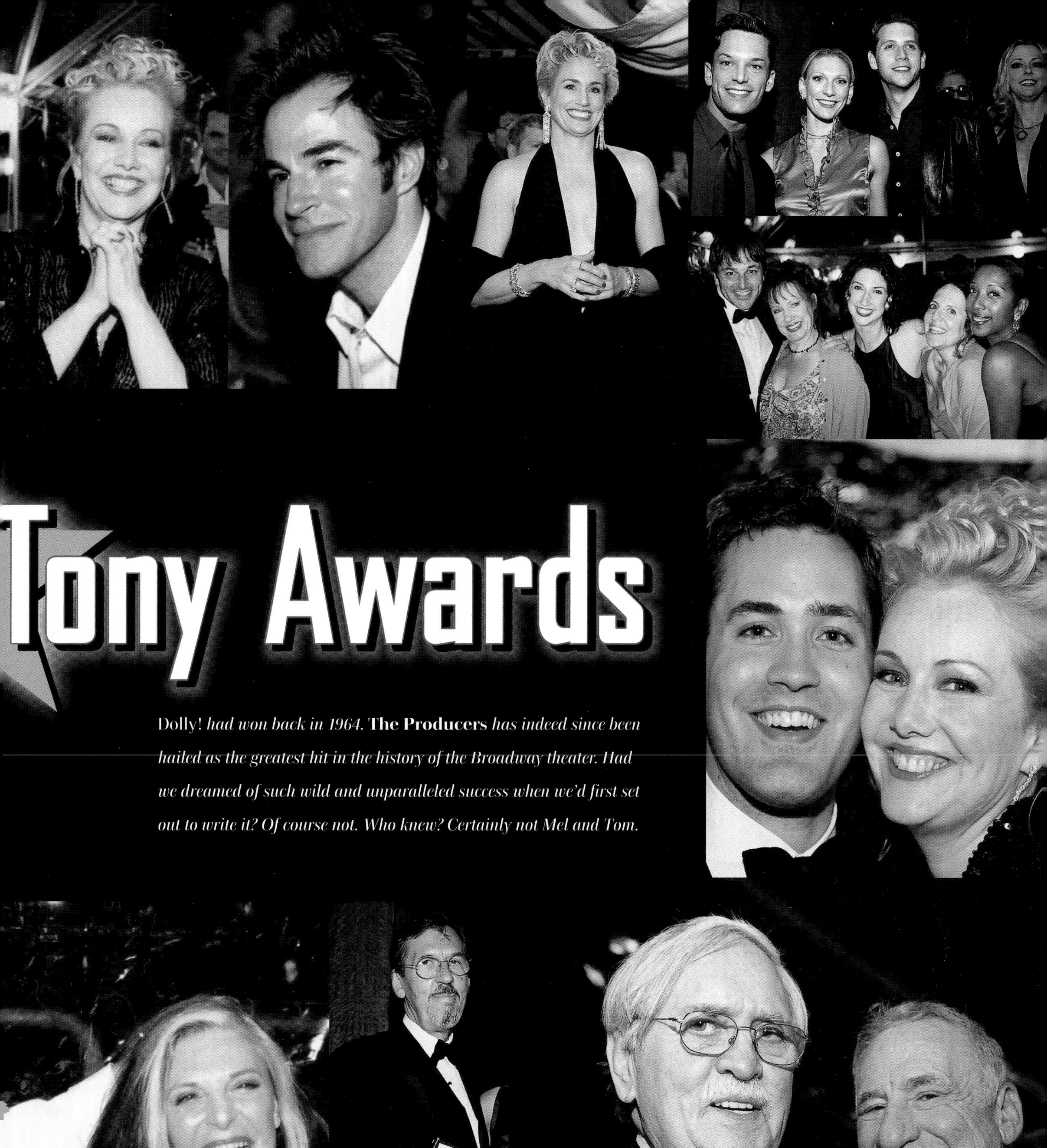

Tony Awards

Dolly! *had won back in 1964.* **The Producers** *has indeed since been hailed as the greatest hit in the history of the Broadway theater. Had we dreamed of such wild and unparalleled success when we'd first set out to write it? Of course not. Who knew? Certainly not Mel and Tom.*

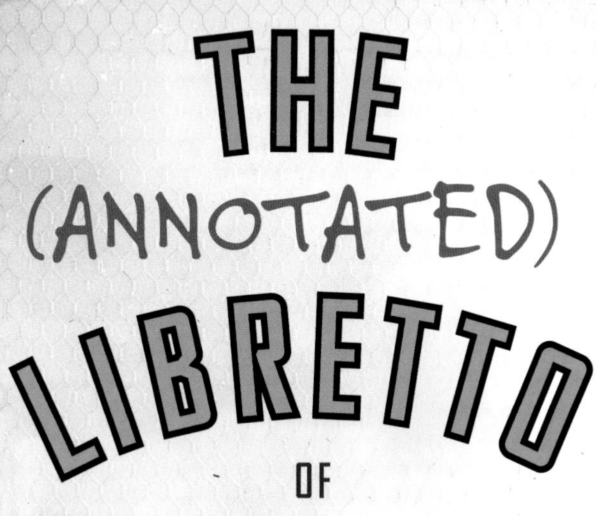
THE
(ANNOTATED)
LIBRETTO
OF
THE PRODUCERS

BOOK BY

MEL BROOKS

AND

TOM MEEHAN

MUSIC & LYRICS BY

MEL BROOKS

MUSICAL ARRANGEMENT BY

GLEN KELLY

DIRECTION AND CHOREOGRAPHY BY

SUSAN STROMAN

CAST

Max Bialystock	Nathan Lane
Leo Bloom	Matthew Broderick
Franz Liebkind	Brad Oscar
Roger De Bris	Gary Beach
Carmen Ghia	Roger Bart
Ulla	Cady Huffman

THE ENSEMBLE

Jeffry Denman, Madeleine Doherty, Bryn Dowling, Kathy Fitzgerald, Robert H. Fowler, Ida Gilliams, Eric Gunhus, Kimberly Hester, Naomi Kakuk, Matt Loehr, Peter Marinos, Angie L. Schworer, Jennifer Smith, Abe Sylvia, Tracy Terstriep, Ray Wills

THE SWINGS

Jim Borstelmann, Adrienne Gibbons, Jamie LaVerdiere, Brad Musgrove, Christina Marie Norrup

SCENES

ACT ONE

Scene 1
Shubert Alley

"Opening Night"

"The King of Broadway"

Scene 2
Max's Office, June 16, 1959

"We Can Do It"

Scene 3
The Chambers Street Offices of Whitehall and Marks

"I Wanna Be a Producer"

Scene 4
Max's Office

"We Can Do It" (Reprise)

Scene 5
Max's Office Early the Following Morning

Scene 6
The Rooftop of a Greenwich Village Apartment Building

"In Old Bavaria"

"Der Guten Tag Hop Clop"

Scene 7
The Living Room of Renowned Theatrical Director Roger De Bris's Elegant East Side Townhouse on a Sunny Tuesday Afternoon in June

"Keep It Gay"

Scene 8
Max's Office

"When You Got It, Flaunt It"

Scene 9
Little Old Lady Land

"Along Came Bialy"

"Act One Finale"

ACT TWO

Scene 1
Max's Office, Late Morning, a Few Weeks Later

"That Face"

Scene 2
The Bare Stage of a Broadway Theater

"Haben Sie Gehoert Das Deutsche Band?"

Scene 3
Shubert Alley

"Opening Night" (Reprise)

"You Never Say 'Good Luck' on Opening Night"

Scene 4
The Stage of the Shubert Theatre

"Springtime for Hitler"

Scene 5
Max's Office, Later That Night

"Where Did We Go Right?"

Scene 6
The Holding Cell of a New York Courthouse, Ten Days Later

"Betrayed"

Scene 7
A New York Courtroom

"'Til Him"

Scene 8
Sing Sing

"Prisoners of Love"

Scene 9
The Stage of the Shubert Theatre

"Prisoners of Love" (Reprise)

Scene 10
Shubert Alley

"Leo and Max"

Curtain Call

"Goodbye!"

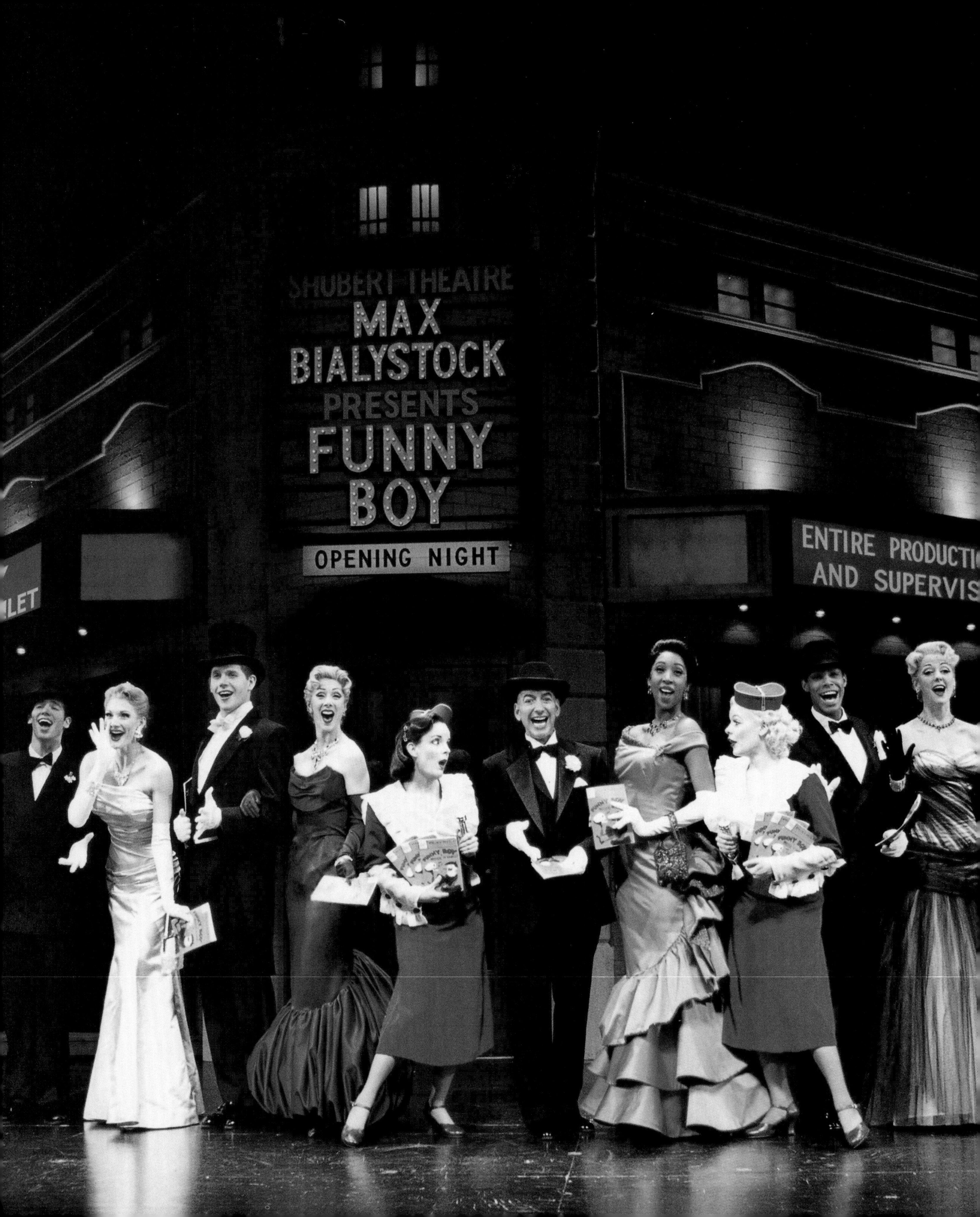

SHUBERT THEATRE
MAX BIALYSTOCK PRESENTS FUNNY BOY
OPENING NIGHT
ENTIRE PRODUCTIO
AND SUPERVIS

ACT ONE - SCENE 1

The OVERTURE *ends and the* CURTAIN *rises on Shubert Alley, with the brightly lit Shubert Theatre upstage center and its stage door upstage left. The time is around 10:30 p.m. on an evening in early June, many many years ago, 1959.*

The marquee of the Shubert says, "Max Bialystock Presents . . . A Max Bialystock Production of FUNNY BOY! *. . . A New Musical Version of* Hamlet *. . . Entire production conceived, devised, thought up, and supervised by Max Bialystock." A sign says, "Opening Night."*

Discovered on stage at rise is a pair of perky and pretty young theater USHERETTES *as* MUSIC *immediately begins under: The introduction to the upcoming song, "Opening Night."*

USHERETTES #1 AND #2 *OPENING NIGHT . . .*
. . . IT'S OPENING NIGHT!
IT'S MAX BIALYSTOCK'S LATEST SHOW,
WILL IT FLOP OR WILL IT GO?

THE CAST IS TAKING ITS FINAL BOW,
HERE COMES THE AUDIENCE NOW!
THE DOORS ARE OPEN;
THEY'RE ON THEIR WAY . . .
LET'S HEAR WHAT THEY HAVE TO SAY!

Originally, in early drafts, we opened with the on-stage finale of Max Bialystock's latest flop, a shameless rip-off of Oklahoma! called Hey, Nebraska!* But we realized that it sounded like something out of an Off Broadway revue and quickly dumped it for a better idea—don't show the rotten show, show the audience's reaction to it.

(* To see the song—and you must—turn the page)

A chorus of FIRST NIGHTERS, *couples in evening clothes, enter, bursting out of the side doors, upstage center, of the Shubert Theatre.*

MEN FIRST NIGHTERS *(bright, all smiles)*

HE'S DONE IT AGAIN,
HE'S DONE IT AGAIN,

WOMEN FIRST NIGHTERS *MAX BIALYSTOCK HAS DONE IT AGAIN!*

ALL *WE CAN'T BELIEVE IT,*
YOU CAN'T CONCEIVE IT . . .

MAN FIRST NIGHTER *HOW'D HE ACHIEVE IT?*

FIRST NIGHTERS *IT'S THE WORST SHOW IN TOWN!*
WE SAT THERE SIGHING,
GROANING AND CRYING,

ALL

OH, WHAT A TERRIBLE EVENING,

OH, WHAT A MISERABLE NIGHT!

LEADING MAN & BEST GAL

THINGS IN THE STATE OF NEBRASKA

NEVER WILL EVER GO RIGHT.

ALL

NEVER WILL EVER GO RIGHT!

NEBRASKA...NEBRASKA...NEBRASKA...

COLDER THAN ALASKA...

NEBRASKA...NEBRASKA...

HEY, NEBRASKA...

WHERE THE LOUSY WEATHER WILL NOT STOP,

WHERE THE CORNFIELDS FLOOD 'TIL YOU DROWN IN MUD,

AND THE HAIL STORMS WIPE OUT HALF THE CROP!

LEADING MAN

HEY, NEBRASKA...

EV'RY DAY MY SWEETIE PIE AND I

ALMOST DIE OF THIRST,

AS THE DROUGHT GROWS WORSE,

WHILE THE VULTURES CIRCLE WAY UP HIGH.

ALL

OH, WE KNOW WE BELONG TO THIS STATE,

AND THIS STATE WE BELONG TO WE HATE.

AND SO WE CRY...

HEY, NEBRASKA YIPPEE-YI

WE'VE HAD ENOUGH OF NEBRASKA,

SO NEBRASKA, GOODBYE!

OH, WE PLOW AND WE PLANT LOTS OF SEEDS,

BUT UP COMES A SHIT-LOAD OF WEEDS!

AND SO WE SAY...

IF WE STAY WE'RE OUT OF LUCK

WE'RE GETTIN' OUT OF NEBRASKA,

IN NEBRASKA, WE'RE STUCK!

ALWAYS DUST STORMS,

DROUGHT AND HAIL STORMS,

ALWAYS UNDER

RAIN AND THUNDER,

CROPS ARE CRAPPY,

NEVER HAPPY...

FULL OF SHEEP SHIT,

WE'RE IN DEEP SHIT!

HEY NEBRASKA,

YOU SUCK!!

"Hey, Nebraska!"
music and lyrics
by Mel Brooks

THERE'S NO DENYING,
IT'S THE WORST SHOW IN TOWN!

WOMEN FIRST NIGHTERS *OH, WE WANTED TO STAND UP AND HISS . . .*

MEN FIRST NIGHTERS *OOH!*

MEN FIRST NIGHTERS *WE'VE SEEN SHIT . . .*

FIRST NIGHTERS *BUT NEVER LIKE THIS!*

(shout)

Max Bialystock has done it again!

THE SONGS WERE ROTTEN,
THE BOOK WAS STINKIN',
WHAT HE DID TO SHAKESPEARE
BOOTH DID TO LINCOLN!

WORKMAN *(up on a ladder, turning over the "Opening Night" sign to reveal a "Closing Night" sign)*

We have these specially made up for Max Bialystock.

FIRST NIGHTERS *WE COULDN'T LEAVE FASTER . . .*

USHERETTES #1 & #2 *WHAT A DISASTER!*

FIRST NIGHTERS AND USHERETTES *WE ARE STILL IN SHOCK,*
WHO PRODUCED THIS SHLOCK?
THAT SLIMY, SLEAZY MAX BIALYSTOCK!

(shout)

What a bum!!

The USHERETTES *and* FIRST NIGHTERS *exit as the* MUSIC *of "Opening Night" plays them off.*

MAX BIALYSTOCK, *a portly man in his fifties, wearing a battered hat and a shiny, worn-out, and ill-fitting tuxedo from yesteryear, with his black bowtie askew, enters from the shadows. His face is at first obscured by a newspaper he is reading as he enters.*

MAX *(lowering the paper and reading aloud from the review he has been scanning)*

The reviews come out a lot faster when the critics leave at intermission. " . . . By the end of *Funny Boy*, Max Bialystock's hopeless musical of *Hamlet*, everybody is dead. They were the lucky ones." And this is the best review we got.

(as a BLIND VIOLINIST *wanders on, playing "The King of Broadway")*

Where did I go wrong? What happened to me? What happened to me?

(to the BLIND VIOLINIST*)*

You're looking at the man . . .

(as the BLIND VIOLINIST *isn't looking at him, physically turning the* VIOLINIST*'s head so that he is looking at him)*

. . . you're looking at the man who once had the biggest name on Broadway. Max Bialystock—thirteen letters!

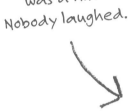

First draft of this line: "You're looking at a man who once had six shows running on Broadway at once—and one of them was a hit!" Nobody laughed.

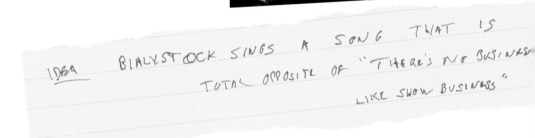

IDEA BIALYSTOCK SINGS A SONG THAT IS TOTAL OPPOSITE OF "THERE'S NO BUSINESS LIKE SHOW BUSINESS"

MAX *sings "The King of Broadway" as the* WORKMAN *and the* BLIND VIOLINIST *stand by and are soon joined by several other late-night theater-district denizens—a* COP*; a* NEWSPAPER VENDOR *toting stacks of newspapers; an aged* BAG LADY*; a slightly drunk* BUM *with a pint of whiskey in a paper bag; two* NUNS *carrying* Playbills *from* The Sound of Music*; a* STREET CLEANER*; and a pair of over-the-hill* STREET WALKERS*. They become a* CHORUS *who join* MAX *in the song and in the middle of the number break out into a Russian/Gypsy dance.*

MAX *I USED TO BE THE KING, THE KING OF OLD BROADWAY,*
THE BEST OF EV'RYTHING WAS MINE TO HAVE EACH DAY.

(up-tempo)

I ALWAYS HAD THE BIGGEST HITS,
THE BIGGEST BATHROOMS AT THE RITZ,
MY SHOWGIRLS HAD THE BIGGEST TITS!
I NEVER WAS THE PITS IN ANY WAY!

WORKMAN, BUM, BAG LADY	*WE BELIEVE YOU, THOUSANDS WOULDN'T,* *WE BELIEVE YOU, EV'RY WORD.* *WE BELIEVE YOU, THOUSANDS COULDN'T,* *WE BELIEVE EACH WORD WE'VE HEARD.*
MAX	*I USED TO BE THE KING . . .*
WORKMAN, BUM, BAG LADY	The King?
MAX	*. . . THE KING OF OLD BROADWAY . . .*
BLIND VIOLINIST	It's good to be the king!
MAX	*MY PRAISES THEY WOULD SING, A ZIEGFELD SO THEY'D SAY.* *(up-tempo)* *MY SHOWS WERE ALWAYS FILLED WITH CLASS,* *THE BEST CHAMPAGNES WOULD FILL MY GLASS,* *MY LAP WAS FILLED WITH GORGEOUS ASS!* *YOU COULDN'T CALL ME CRASS IN ANY WAY!*
WORKMAN, BUM, BAG LADY, VIOLINIST, USHERETTES, NUNS, STREET CLEANER	*WE BELIEVE YOU, THOUSANDS WOULDN'T,* *WE BELIEVE YOU, EV'RY WORD.* *WE BELIEVE YOU, THOUSANDS COULDN'T,* *WE BELIEVE EACH WORD WE'VE HEARD.*
MAX	*THERE WAS A TIME,* *WHEN I WAS YOUNG AND GAY . . .* But straight. *THERE WAS A TIME* *WHEN I WAS BOLD.* *THERE WAS A TIME* *WHEN EACH AND EV'RY PLAY* *I TOUCHED* *WOULD TURN TO GOLD.*
CHORUS	*THERE WAS A TIME,* *HE WORE THE FINEST CLOTHES,* *HIS SHOES WERE ALWAYS NEW.* *AHH!*

Either homage to or stolen from—whichever you prefer—Mel as King Louis XVI in History of the World, Part One.

MAX	*NOW I WEAR A RENTED TUX*	CHORUS	*AAH!*
	THAT'S TWO WEEKS OVERDUE!		*OOH!*

CHORUS	*POOR BIALY, WHAT A SHMOOZER,*	MAX	*RENTED TUX*
	POOR BIALY, WHAT A SHAME.		*OVERDUE*
	POOR BIALY, WHAT A LOSER,		*WAY*
	POOR BIALY, GOODBYE FAME.		*OVERDUE*

MAX *(speaks as* MUSIC *continues under)*

Such reviews! How dare they insult me in this manner? How quickly they forget. I'm Max Bialystock! I was the first producer ever to do summer stock in the winter!

CHORUS *ONCE HE WAS THE KING . . .*

MAX You've heard of theater in the round? You're looking at the man who invented theater in the square! Nobody had a good seat!

CHORUS *. . . KING OF OLD BROADWAY.*

MAX I've spent my entire life in the theatre. I was a protégé of the great Boris Tomaschevski.

CHORUS *OOH!*

LEGATO —

THERE WAS A TIME
WHEN I WAS YOUNG AND GAY

... BUT STRAIGHT

THERE WAS A TIME
WHEN I WAS BOLD

THERE WAS A TIME
WHEN BACH AND EVERY PLAY I TOUCHED
WOULD TURN TO GOLD

THAT TIME

BACH
EVERY BLOCK
ROUND THE CLOCK
CROCK
DOCK
FLOCK
HOCK
JOCK
LOCK
MOCK
KNOCK
ROCK
SOCK
STOCK
SHOCK
TICK-TOCK
YOCK

MAX Yes. He taught me everything I know. I'll never forget, he turned to me on his deathbed and said, "Maxella, alle menschen muss zu machen, jeden tug a gantzen kachen, pichin peepee kakan!"

NOT written by us, but brilliantly ad-libbed by Nathan Lane in rehearsal. Since it's gotten a huge laugh at every show, we've taken full credit for it.

NUN #1 What does that mean?

MAX Who knows? I don't speak Yiddish. Strangely enough, neither did he. But in my heart I knew what he was saying. He was saying, when you're down and out, and everybody thinks you're finished, that's the time to stand up on your two feet and shout, "Who do you have to fuck to get a break in this town?!"

CHORUS Yay!

MAX and the CHORUS do a wild kind of Russian/Gypsy dance.

MAX *(sings, following the dance)*

MAX	CHORUS
I USED TO BE THE KING	*AH, USED TO BE THE KING*
THE KING OF OLD BROADWAY,	*KING OF OLD BROADWAY*
AGAIN I WILL BE KING	*AHH*
AND BE ON TOP TO STAY.	*ON TOP TO STAY, HEY!*

(up-tempo)

THERE'LL BE GALA
OPENING NIGHTS AGAIN,
YOU'LL SEE MY NAME IN
LIGHTS AGAIN,

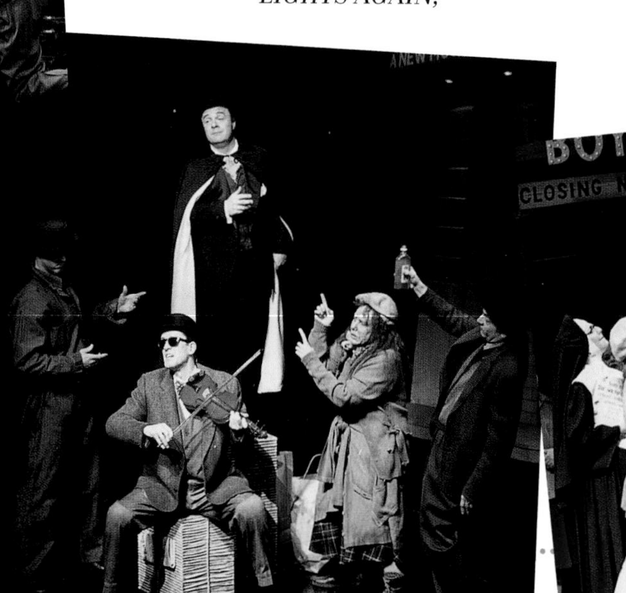

PRESENTS
FUNNY BOY
CLOSING NIGHT
ENTIRE PRODUCT
AND SUPERVI

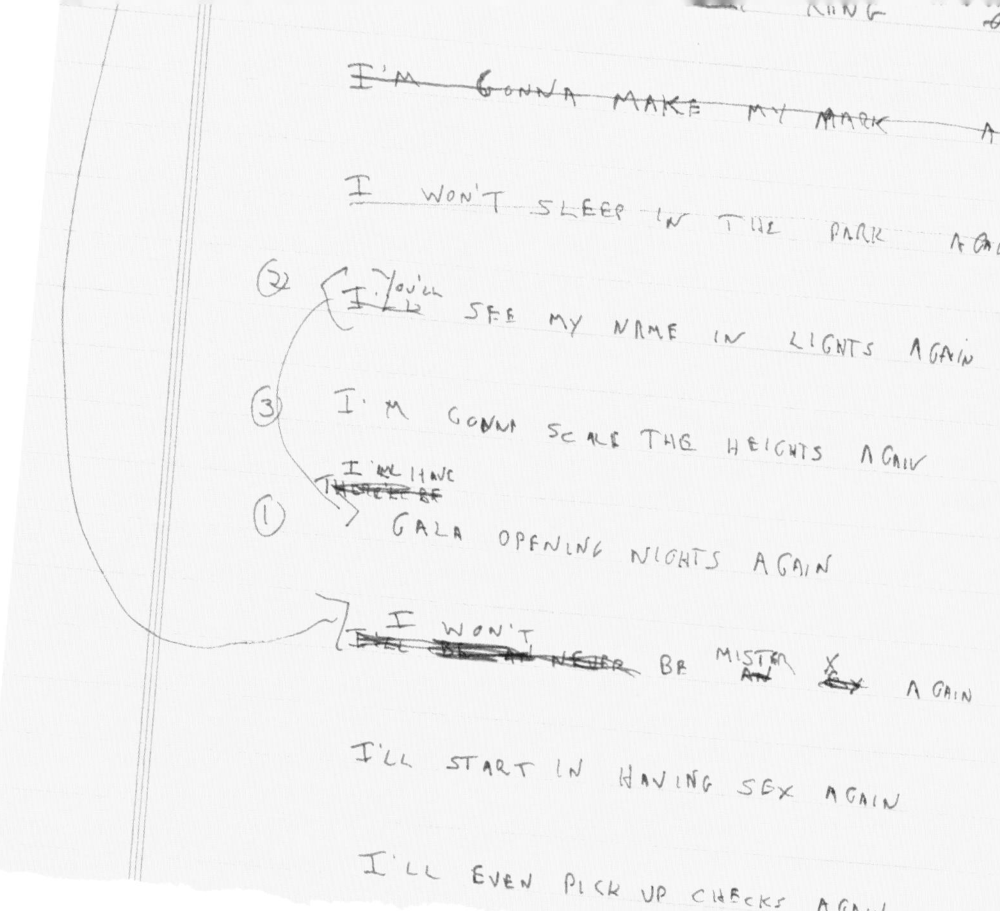

I'LL GO FROM DARK
TO BRIGHTS AGAIN!
MY SPIRITS HIGH
AS KITES AGAIN,
I'LL NEVER SUFFER
SLIGHTS AGAIN,
I'LL TASTE THOSE SWEET
DELIGHTS AGAIN!
NO PLETHORA OF
PLIGHTS AGAIN,
NO BLOSSOMING OF
BLIGHTS AGAIN,
NO FRANTIC FITS OR
FRIGHTS AGAIN!
FAME IS IN MY
SIGHTS AGAIN,
I'LL TAKE THOSE FANCY
FLIGHTS AGAIN,
I'M GONNA SCALE THE
HEIGHTS AGAIN!

BIALYSTOCK WILL		
NEVER DROP,	CHORUS	*AHH*
BIALYSTOCK WILL		
NEVER STOP . . .		*AHH*
BIALYSTOCK WILL		*FAME IS IN HIS SIGHTS AGAIN*
BE ON TOP AGAIN		*HE'LL TAKE THOSE FANCY FLIGHTS AGAIN*

(holding the final note until the CHORUS *almost finishes its section)*

	HE'S GONNA SCALE THE HEIGHTS AGAIN
I'LL BE ON TOP AGAIN, HEY!	*HE'LL BE ON TOP AGAIN, HEY!*

The end of the number marks the end of Scene 1 as the CHORUS *exits while* MUSIC *plays under,* LIGHTS *change,* SCENERY *begins to move, and we segue into Scene 2.*

ACT ONE - SCENE 2

MAX's office. Perhaps once grand but now shabby and cluttered, as in the movie. There is a large desk, a couple of chairs, an old brown upright piano near the entrance door to the office, stage right, and a large black safe next to a small refrigerator on the floor against the wall stage left. There is also evidence that MAX is living in his office—i.e., we see things like a hot plate, a coffee maker, and a line of underwear and socks hung up to dry. There is a large old leather sofa stage center and, behind it, stage left, a door that leads to a bathroom. A pair of French doors, upstage right and upstage left, lead out onto a balcony. There are two closets in the office—a coat closet and a utility closet containing scripts, etc. There is also a coatrack. Lettering on the office door says, "Max Bialystock, Theatrical Producer." A half-dozen or so framed posters of former Bialystock productions—including When Cousins Marry *and* The Breaking Wind*—decorate the walls of the office. The time is a month or so later, Wednesday, June 16th, around eleven a.m. MAX lies down on the sofa. We hear a timid knocking at the door, downstage right. The door opens and LEOPOLD BLOOM peers in. He is a meek-mannered accountant in his mid-thirties, wearing a ratty raincoat over a thirty-five-dollar Robert Hall suit, and is carrying a cheap looks-like-leather plastic briefcase.*

In chicago, he wore a suit that made him look like Tyrone Power in The Eddie Duchin Story. We changed the suit for a nerdier version.

LEO Hello, Mr. Bialystock?

(taking a couple of steps in)

Anybody here? Mr. Bialystock?

MAX *(jumping up from the sofa; bellowing, scaring LEO half to death)*

Who are you? What are you doing here? What do you want? Speak to me, dummy. Speak! Why don't you speak?

LEO Scared. Can't talk.

MAX Get a hold of yourself. Take a deep breath.

LEO Aaaaaaaaaaaah.

MAX Who are you?

LEO I'm Leopold Bloom. I'm an accountant. I'm from Whitehall and Marks. I've come here to do your books.

MAX You have, huh? Well . . .

(SOUND: a knock on the door)

Who is it?

HOLD ME–TOUCH ME *(from off-stage)*

Hold me. Touch me.

MAX Hold Me–Touch Me. One of my backers.

(pushing LEO toward the bathroom door)

Listen, I have to meet with an important investor. Go to the bathroom.

LEO I don't have to go.

MAX Try, try. Think of Niagara Falls.

(MAX pushes LEO into the bathroom as there is another knock on the door)

Be with you in a moment, my darling.

MAX *hurries to a corner cabinet that he opens to reveal the framed photographs of several dozen* LITTLE OLD LADIES. *He hastily hunts through them, looking for* HOLD ME–TOUCH ME *while mumbling aloud to himself.*

MAX Lemme see, where is Hold Me–Touch Me, Hold Me–Touch Me? Kiss Me–Feel Me, Clinch Me–Pinch Me, Lick Me–Bite Me, Suck Me–F . . . ah, yes, here she is, Hold Me–Touch Me.

He grabs HOLD ME–TOUCH ME*'s photograph from the cabinet, closes the cabinet, and holds the large, framed 8" by 10" photograph, places it on the piano, and heads to answer the door. At that moment, however,* LEO *comes out of the bathroom.*

LEO *(zipping his fly)*

You know, it worked, as soon as I pictured Niagara Falls, I . . .

MAX *(in a loud whisper; hastily shoving* LEO *back into the bathroom and closing the door on him)*

Back, back! Don't make a sound. And don't listen to anything you hear.

(he hurries to the office door and opens it to reveal HOLD ME-TOUCH ME *standing there with an umbrella in hand. She is a woman of eighty or so, a quintessential little old lady)*

Sweetheart.

HOLD ME–TOUCH ME Hold me. Touch me.

MAX As soon as I shut the door.

HOLD ME–TOUCH ME What's the matter, Bialy? Don't you love me?

MAX Love you? I adore you. Did you bring the checkee? Bialy can't produce play-ees without check-ees.

HOLD ME–TOUCH ME *(taking out a check, starting to hand it to him, and then yanking it back, just out of his grasp)*

Here you go . . . but first, could we please play a game, one dirty little game?

MAX All right, you devil woman. What'll it be, "The Debutante and the Bricklayer"?

HOLD ME–TOUCH ME No.

MAX "The Rabbi and the Contortionist"? You like that one.

HOLD ME–TOUCH ME *(as* LEO *once again starts out of the bathroom, behind her back, so that she doesn't see him)*

No. Oh, I know, let's play "The Virgin Milkmaid and the Well-Hung Stable Boy."

MAX I don't think I have the strength.

HOLD ME–TOUCH ME Don't worry, I'll be gentle.

(using her umbrella to represent a yoke on which she is pretending to carry two pails of milk)

Oooh, this milk is sooo heavy. I'll never reach the house. Help. Help. Oh, you there, Well-Hung Stable Boy, won't you help me?

MAX Of course, my little Dairy Queen. First I'll take your milk and then I'll take your virginity.

HOLD ME–TOUCH ME *(as* MAX *grabs her and holds her close)*

No, no! Never, never! Yes, yes! Give it to me, Well-Hung, give it to me!

MAX Easy!

LEO *(stepping out of the bathroom)*

Omigod.

MAX You mean "oops," don't you? Just say "oops" and go back in there!

LEO Ahhhhahhhhhhhahhhh.

MAX Not "ahhhhahhhahhh"—"oops."

LEO Oops.

HOLD ME–TOUCH ME *(grabbing* MAX *back into her arms)*

Send me to the moon, you animal. Send me to the moon!

MAX Yes, yes, my darling. Thursday. Come back Thursday. I'll send you to the moon on Thursday. I may even join you. But, right now, please, the checkee. Get the checkee.

HOLD ME–TOUCH ME Checkee! Oh, yes. Here. I made it out like you told me. To the title of the play. Cash. That's a funny name for a play. Cash.

Before we hit on The Iceman, we went for another O'Neill play, Strange Interlude, smart because they'd just had a strange interlude, but no laugh. Mel suggested Under the Yum-Yum Tree, but the consensus was that nobody but Mel had ever heard of it.

MAX So is *The Iceman Cometh.* See ya Thursday. Goodbye, my pouter-pigeon. Ta-ta.

HOLD ME–TOUCH ME Goodbye, ta-ta.

MAX Ta-ta. Bye-bye.

(she exits. He pockets the check and mutters)

You dirty old buzzard.

LEO May I come out of the bathroom now, Mr. Bialystock?

MAX Yeah, yeah, all right.

LEO *(coming timidly out of the bathroom)*

I'm terribly sorry that I caught you feeling up the old lady.

MAX Caught me "feeling up the old lady." Thank you, Mr. Tact. May I take your coat?

LEO Thank you.

MAX So you're an accountant, huh?

LEO Yes, sir, I am, sir.

MAX Then account for yourself! Do you believe in God? Do you believe in gold? Why are you looking up old ladies' dresses? A bit of a pervert, huh?

LEO Oh!

MAX I know what you're thinking. How dare you condemn me without knowing all the facts?

LEO Mr. Bialystock, I'm not con . . .

MAX Shut up! I'm having a rhetorical conversation. Do you know who I used to be?

LEO Yes, you're Max Bialystock. The king of Broadway.

MAX No! I'm Max Bialy–! That's right. That's right.

LEO May I say, Mr. Bialystock, you're not just a dirty old man . . .

Before we got to this, we tried Skirts Ahoy and Old Faces of 1952.

MAX Thank you.

LEO . . . you're also a great Broadway producer. And there's something about me you should know. I had the good fortune, when I was a kid, to be taken to *Bialy-Hoos of 1942*. I still have the ticket stub, and ever since I've had this secret desire to be a Broadway producer.

(MUSIC: *Out*)

MAX A secret desire, huh? Well, kid, let me give you a little advice.

LEO Yes.

MAX Keep it a secret. Do the books, do the books.

LEO Yes, sir.

(he sits and begins doing the books as MAX *wanders over to the French door, upstage left, and gazes idly out)*

MAX Oh, my God, will you look at that. There's a great big gorgeous blonde stepping out of a white Rolls Royce limo.

(flinging open the French door and shouting out to the street below)

That's it, baby, when you got it, flaunt it! Flaunt it! Ha ha.

(closing the French door and stepping back into the room)

LEO Mr. Bialystock. May I speak to you for a minute?

MAX What, a minute?

LEO Yes, a minute.

MAX *(getting up and pulling out a pocket watch)*

Okay. One minute.

LEO In glancing at . . . .

MAX Go. You have 58 seconds left. You've wasted two seconds.

LEO Well, in glancing at your books, I notice that in the columns marked . . .

MAX You have 48 seconds left, hurry, hurry.

LEO *(flustered)*

Oh! Uh, in the columns marked monies received . . .

MAX 28 seconds. You're running out of time.

Tick-tock. Tick-tock.
Tick-tock. Tick-tock.

17 seconds. 15 seconds.

LEO There's a discrepancy between the figures

I can't make the figures add up . . . .

If I can just have a moment I think I can explain . . .

LEO, beyond the point of endurance, gets up from the desk and pulls a piece of blue material from his pants pocket.

LEO Mr. Bialystock, I cannot function under these conditions. You're making me extremely nervous.

MAX What is that? A handkerchief?

LEO What? Nothing. It's nothing.

MAX *(grabbing the material from LEO)*

If it's nothing, why can't I see it?

LEO *(reaching for the material to get it back from MAX)*

My blanket! My blanket! My blue blanket. Give me back my blue blanket!

(mumbling, moaning)

MAX *(giving the blue blanket back)*

Shhh. Here, here, here, here.

(patting LEO*'s face with both hands, trying to calm him)*

Don't panic. Don't panic.

LEO Ahhhhhhh. I'm sorry. I don't like people touching my blue blanket. It's not important. It's a minor compulsion. I can deal with it if I want to. It's just that I've had it ever since I was a baby and I find it very comforting . . . I need to lie down for a minute.

(he gets down on the floor and curls up in the fetal position, moaning to himself)

MAX They come here. They all come here. How do they find me?

(crossing to stand towering over him, leaning down to help him up)

How can I help you?

LEO *(terrified)*

Ahhhhhh! You're going to jump on me!

MAX What?

LEO You're going to jump on me. I know you're going to jump on me and squash me like a bug! Please don't jump on me!

MAX *(jumping up and down)*

I'm not going to jump on you! I'm not going to jump on you! Will you please get a hold of yourself?

(once again putting out a hand to help him up)

LEO *(scrambling to his feet and backing away from* MAX*: hysterical)*

Don't touch me! Don't touch me!

MAX Stop that! What's the matter with you?

LEO I'm hysterical. I'm having hysterics. I'm hysterical. I can't stop. When I get like this, I can't stop. I'm hysterical.

MAX I can see that.

(during the above, MAX *rushes to his desk, pours a cup of water, rushes back, and tosses the water in* LEO*'s face)*

LEO I'm wet! I'm wet! I'm hysterical and I'm wet!

*(*MAX *slaps* LEO *across the face)*

I'm in pain! I'm in pain! And I'm wet! And I'm still hysterical!

MAX What can I do? What can I do? You're getting me hysterical!

LEO You're too close. Go away. Go away. You frighten me. Sit down over there.

MAX *(crossing to sit at the desk and giving* LEO *a forced nice-guy, twinkle-eyed, touchy-feely smile)*

I'm sitting! How's this?

LEO That's good. That's very nice. I think I'm coming out of it now.

(as MAX *flashes an even broader and phonier smile)*

Thank you for smiling, that helped a great deal.

MAX Well, you know what they say, "Smile and the world smiles with you." Heh, heh, heh, heh.

(to himself)

This man should be in a straitjacket.

(again flashing his phoniest smile)

Feeling better?

LEO *(calmed down, putting away his blue blanket)*

Yes, I'm fine now. Thank you. May I speak to you?

MAX Yes, Prince Mishkin, what can we do for you?

Dostoevsky's idiot in The Idiot, suggesting here that Bloom is an idiot. The line's from the movie—Mel's films are peppered with allusions to literary classics.

LEO This is hardly the time for levity, Mr. Bialystock. I've discovered a serious error here in the accounts of your last show, *Funny Boy.*

MAX Where? What?

LEO According to the backers' list, you raised a hundred thousand dollars. But the show only cost ninety-eight thousand. There's two thousand dollars unaccounted for.

MAX So I went to a Turkish bath, who cares? The show was a flop. Bloom, do me a favor, move a few decimal points around. You can do it. You're an accountant. You're in a noble profession. The word "count" is part of your title.

LEO That's cheating.

MAX It's not cheating. It's charity.

(thrusting his stickpin close to LEO*'s eye)*

You see this stickpin? This once held a pearl as big as your eye. Bloom, I used to wear handmade Italian shoes, five-hundred-dollar suits, and look at me now, look at me now . . . I'm wearing a cardboard belt! Bloom, I'm reaching out to you. Don't send me to prison. Help!

LEO All right . . . I'll do it, I'll do it. Let's see, two thousand dollars. Two thousand dollars isn't that much. I am sure that I can hide it somewhere. After all, the IRS isn't interested in a show that flopped.

We wanted a lightbulb literally to go off. We even discussed putting a table right behind the couch with a lamp on it. Mel actually did it with Sid Caesar in Silent Movie. Mel pitches a great idea for a movie to save the studio, and when Sid Caesar, as studio chief, gets it, a lightbulb goes on behind his head. Got a big laugh in the movie.

MAX Right, good thinking. You figure it out.

(crossing to the couch)

I'm gonna take a little nap. If anybody calls, I'm not in. Unless it's Yank Me–Spank Me.

LEO *(to himself as* MAX *seems to fall sleep)*

Now, let's see . . . if we add these deductions, we get, ah, hmmm . . . amazing . . . it's absolutely amazing, but under the right circumstances, a producer could make more money with a flop than he could with a hit.

*(*MUSIC: *Sting.* MAX *abruptly awakens and sits halfway up as he hears what* LEO *has said;* MUSIC *continues under the following dialogue up to the song "We Can Do It")*

Hmmmm. Yes. It's quite possible. If he were certain that the show would fail, a man could make a fortune.

MAX *(rising and moving slowly toward* LEO*)*

Yes?

LEO Yes, what?

MAX Yes, what you were saying. Keep talking.

LEO What was I saying?

MAX You were saying that, under the right circumstances, a producer could make more money with a flop than he could with a hit.

LEO Yes, it's quite possible.

MAX You keep saying that, but you don't say how!

LEO Well, it's simply a matter of creative accounting. Let's assume, just for the moment, that you are a dishonest man.

MAX Assume away.

LEO All right. When you produced your last show, *Funny Boy,* you raised two thousand dollars more than you needed. But you could've raised a million, put on your hundred-thousand-dollar flop, *Funny Boy,* and kept the rest.

MAX But what if my show was a hit?

LEO Well, then you go to jail. See, instead of a hundred percent of the show, you will have sold more than a thousand percent. And so if it's a hit, you can't pay off the backers. Get it?

MAX Got it. So in order for our scheme to work we'd have to find a sure-fire flop.

Mel's universe was turned on this thought. It led him to write the film The Producers. It turned a young man's hope into a big career.

LEO Our scheme? What scheme?

MAX What scheme? Your scheme, you bloody little genius.

LEO I meant no scheme. I merely posed a little academic accounting theory. It was just a thought.

MAX Bloom, worlds are turned on such thoughts. Don't you see, Bloom. Darling Bloom, glorious Bloom. It's so simple. Step One: We find the worst play ever written. Step Two: We hire the worst director in town. Step Three: I raise two million dollars . . .

LEO Two?

MAX Yes! One for me, one for you. There's a lot of little old ladies out there. Step Four: We hire the worst actors in New York and open on Broadway. And before you can say Step Five we close on Broadway, take our two million, and go to Rio.

LEO Rio? No, it would never work.

MAX Oh ye of little faith.

WHAT DID LEWIS SAY TO CLARK
WHEN EVERYTHING LOOKED BLEAK?
WHAT DID SIR EDMUND SAY TO TENZING
AS THEY STRUGGLED TOWARD EVEREST'S PEAK?
WHAT DID WASHINGTON SAY TO HIS TROOPS
AS THEY CROSSED THE DELAWARE,
I'M SURE YOU'RE WELL AWARE . . .

LEO What did they say?

MAX *WE CAN DO IT, WE CAN DO IT,*
WE CAN DO IT, ME AND YOU.
WE CAN DO IT, WE CAN DO IT,
WE CAN MAKE OUR DREAMS COME TRUE.
EVERYTHING YOU'VE EVER WANTED
IS JUST WAITING TO BE HAD.
BEAUTIFUL GIRLS, WEARING NOTHING BUT PEARLS,
CARESSING YOU, UNDRESSING YOU,
AND DRIVING YOU MAD.

WE CAN DO IT, WE CAN DO IT,
THIS IS NOT THE TIME TO SHIRK.
WE CAN DO IT, YOU WON'T RUE IT,
SAY GOODBYE TO PETTY CLERK.
HI, PRODUCER; YES, PRODUCER,
I MEAN YOU, SIR, GO BERSERK!
WE CAN DO IT, WE CAN DO IT,
AND I KNOW IT'S GONNA WORK!

Whatta ya say, Bloom?

LEO *WHAT DO I SAY,*
FINALLY A CHANCE TO BE A BROADWAY PRODUCER!
WHAT DO I SAY?
FINALLY A CHANCE TO MAKE MY DREAMS COME TRUE, SIR!
WHAT DO I SAY, WHAT DO I SAY,
HERE'S WHAT I SAY TO YOU, SIR . . .

(mournful, frightened)

I CAN'T DO IT, I CAN'T DO IT,
I CAN'T DO IT, THAT'S NOT ME.

I'M A LOSER, I'M A COWARD,
I'M A CHICKEN, DON'T YOU SEE?

WHEN IT COMES TO WOOING WOMEN,
THERE'S A FEW THINGS THAT I LACK.

BEAUTIFUL GIRLS, WEARING NOTHING BUT PEARLS,
CHASING ME, EMBRACING ME,
I'D HAVE AN ATTACK.

MAX You miserable, cowardly, wretched little caterpillar! Don't you ever want to become a butterfly? Don't you want to spread your wings and flap your way to glory?

MAX *WE CAN DO IT,*
WE CAN DO IT . . .

WE CAN GRAB THAT
HOLY
GRAIL.

LEO *MR. BIALYSTOCK,*
PLEASE STOP THE
SONG,
YOU GOT ME WRONG,
I'LL SAY "SO LONG,"
I'M NOT AS
STRONG
A PERSON AS YOU
THINK!

MAX *WE CAN DO IT,*
WE CAN DO IT . . .
DRINK
CHAMPAGNE
NOT
GINGER ALE!
COME ON, LEO,
CAN'T YOU SEE-O . . .

LEO *MR. BIALYSTOCK,*
JUST TAKE A LOOK,
I'M NOT A CROOK,
I'M JUST A SHNOOK,
THE BOTTOM LINE
IS THAT I STINK!
I . . . CAN'T . . . DO . . . IT!

LEO *YOU SEE RIO, I SEE JAIL!*

MAX *WE CAN DO IT!*

LEO *I CAN'T DO IT!*

MAX *WE CAN DO IT!*

LEO *I CANNOT, CANNOT, CANNOT, CANNOT DO IT,*

'CAUSE I KNOW IT'S GONNA . . .
FAIL.

MAX Fail! Fail? It can't miss. All you need is a little courage. Bloom, you're like a fountain waiting to explode and shoot up to the sky.

LEO I'm a fountain?

MAX Yes, don't you realize, there's a lot more to you than there is to you.

LEO *(getting his briefcase and putting on his raincoat)*

I'm sorry, Mr. Bialystock, I'm afraid you've made a terrible error in judgment. You've mistaken me for someone with a spine. I'm going back to Whitehall and Marks. Goodbye forever!

(he exits)

MAX Oh . . . oh . . .

(sinking to his knees and shouting)

OH, LORD, I WANT THAT MONEY!!

The "Unhappy" MUSIC *begins as* MAX *freezes on his knees.* LIGHTS *and* SCENERY *change, and we segue into Scene 3.*

ACT ONE - SCENE 3

The Chambers Street offices of Whitehall and Marks, LEO'*s employers. A little later the same day.*

A row of six desks, at each of which sits a dispirited ACCOUNTANT *working at an old-fashioned, hand-cranked adding machine. The* ACCOUNTANTS *work silently, pulling the side levers on their adding machines in a clicking unison. It is like a scene out of an Expressionist silent German movie or out of Elmer Rice's* The Adding Machine. *Rhythmic, tuneless* MUSIC *underscores.*

ACCOUNTANTS *(groan)*

OH.
UNHAPPY . . . UNHAPPY . . . VERY UNHAPPY.
UNHAPPY . . . UNHAPPY . . . VERY VERY VERY VERY VERY
VERY VERY UNHAPPY . . .

God bless Glen Kelly; he had the idea for the "unhappy" section.

Now, LEO *nervously enters downstage left, timidly makes his way to his front-row desk. His boss,* MARKS, *a short-tempered, cigar-chomping little tyrant, is standing right next to his desk.*

MARKS *(shouting as* LEO *enters)*

Bloom!!!

(at the explosive sound of his name, LEO *frightenedly jumps)*

Where the hell have you been?! You're six minutes late. This is an accounting firm, not a country club. You can't come and go as you please.

LEO *(as he picks up his things)*

Yes, Mr. Marks.

MARKS Remember, you're a nobody, a PA, a Public Accountant. And I am a CPA, a Certified Public Accountant—a rank that a miserable little worm like you can never hope to achieve.

LEO Yes, Mr. Marks.

MARKS *(to* ALL*)*

You, what are you gawking at? You never saw a person humiliated before? Get back to work, all of you!

(he exits)

LEO AND THE ACCOUNTANTS *(in unison, as they all go back to work)*

UNHAPPY . . . UNHAPPY . . .
VERY VERY VERY VERY VERY VERY VERY VERY . . .
UNHAPPY.

BLACK MAN ACCOUNTANT *(sings mournfully, "Old Man River"-style)*

OH, I DEBITS ALL DE MORNIN',
AN' I CREDITS ALL DE EB'NIN',
UNTIL DEM LEDGERS BE RIGHTTTT . . .

LEO AND THE ACCOUNTANTS *UNTIL DEM LEDGERS BE RIGHTTTT!*

LEO *suddenly stops working. Music of "I Wanna Be a Producer" begins.*

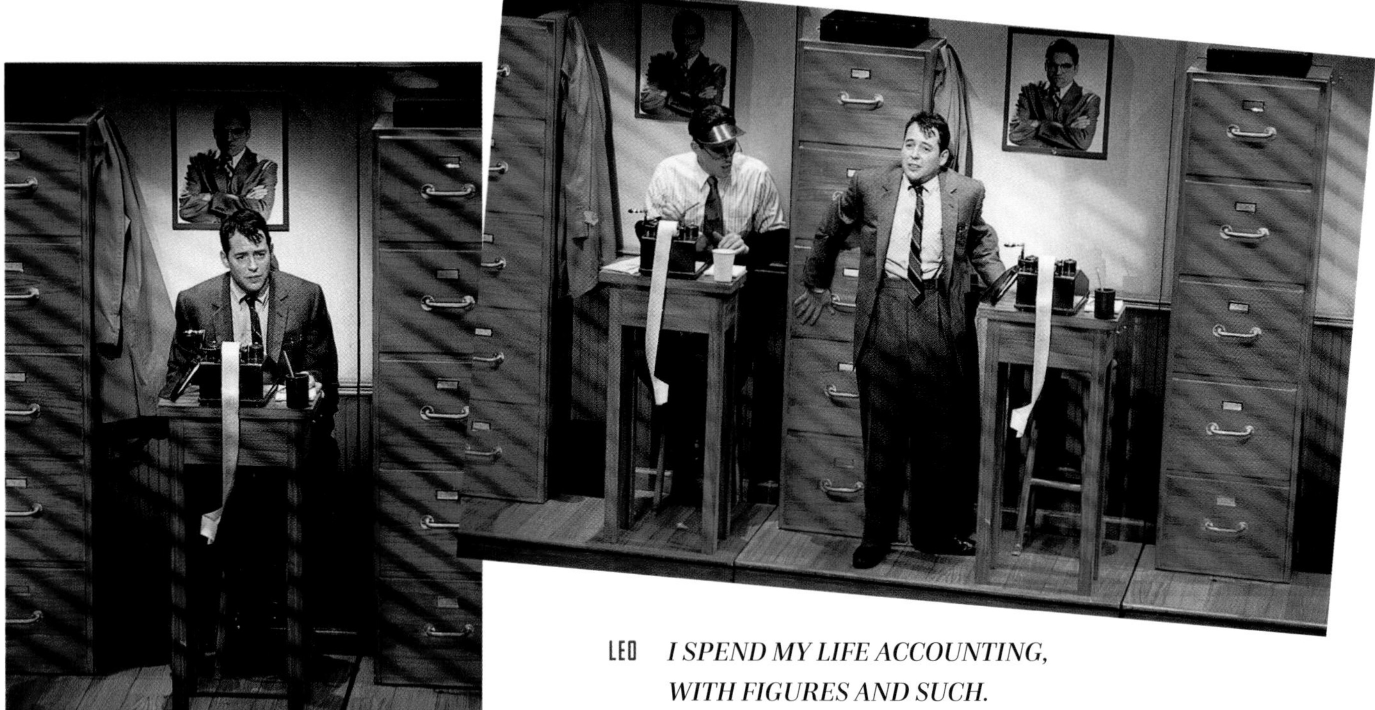

LEO	*I SPEND MY LIFE ACCOUNTING,* *WITH FIGURES AND SUCH.*
ACCOUNTANTS	*UNHAPPY.*
LEO	*TO WHAT IS MY LIFE AMOUNTING,* *IT FIGURES, NOT MUCH.*
ACCOUNTANTS	*UNHAPPY.*
LEO	*I HAVE A SECRET DESIRE* *HIDING DEEP IN MY SOUL,* *IT SETS MY HEART AFIRE* *TO SEE ME IN THIS ROLE . . .*

Now, in a fantasy sequence that is presumably all in LEO*'s mind,* LEO *gets up from his desk, grabs a top hat and cane out of a file cabinet, and begins singing and dancing to "I Wanna Be a Producer."*

LEO	*(he sings and dances)* *I WANNA BE A PRODUCER* *WITH A BIG SHOW ON BROADWAY.* *I WANNA BE A PRODUCER,* *LUNCH AT SARDI'S EVERY DAY.* *I WANNA BE A PRODUCER,* *SPORT A TOP HAT AND A CANE.*

Our musical conductor, Patrick Brady, decided to break the word cane into two syllables (cay-ane) to give it a vaudeville sound. Matthew loved the idea and does it beautifully every night.

I WANNA BE A PRODUCER
AND DRIVE THOSE CHORUS GIRLS INSANE!

Now, several gorgeous CHORUS GIRLS *in sexy short skirts—appearing from nowhere out of filing cabinets—join him in the number.*

LEO *I WANNA BE A PRODUCER*
AND SLEEP UNTIL
HALF-PAST TWO. CHORUS GIRLS *OOH!*

I WANNA BE A PRODUCER
AND SAY, "YOU, YOU, YOU,
NOT YOU."

On NOT YOU, LEO *indicates a* CHORUS GIRL *who exits in shame.*

I WANNA BE A
PRODUCER,
WEAR A TUX ON
OP'NING NIGHTS!

I WANNA BE A
PRODUCER
AND SEE MY NAME "LEO
BLOOM" IN LIGHTS!

Now the office set splits in the middle and goes off as upstage is magically transformed into a glitzy dream of Broadway featuring a lighted sign saying "Leo Bloom Presents."

LEO *and the* CHORUS GIRLS *do an instrumental tap section.*

CHORUS GIRLS *(singing and continuing to dance following the tap section)*

HE WANTS TO BE
A PRODUCER

LEO Sell it, girls!

CHORUS GIRLS *OF A GREAT BIG BROADWAY SMASH!*

LEO Don't forget the balcony!

CHORUS GIRLS *HE WANTS TO BE A PRODUCER,*
EV'RY POCKET STUFFED WITH CASH!
HE WANTS TO BE A PRODUCER,
PINCH OUR CHEEKS 'TIL WE CRY.

CHORUS GIRL #1 Ouch!

CHORUS GIRL #2 Eek!

CHORUS GIRL #3 Ooh!

CHORUS GIRL #4 Oh!

CHORUS GIRL #5 Aah!

CHORUS GIRL #6 Yes!

CHORUS GIRLS *HE WANTS TO BE A PRODUCER*
WITH A GREAT BIG CASTING COUCH!

A water cooler and tray of glasses now enter with pink champagne in place of water. MARKS *enters.*

MARKS Oh, Mr. Bloom!

CHORUS GIRLS Aah!

MARKS *exits.* ALL *"drink" from champagne glasses during the following.*

LEO *I WANNA BE . . .*

CHORUS GIRLS *HE WANTS TO BE . . .*

LEO *I WANNA BE . . .*

CHORUS GIRLS *HE WANTS TO BE . . .*

LEO *I WANNA BE THE GREATEST, GRANDEST,*
AND MOST FABULOUS PRODUCER IN THE WORLD.

CHORUS GIRLS *HE WANTS TO BE A PRODUCER,*
HE WANTS TO DINE WITH A DUCHESS AND A DUKE.

LEO *I JUST GOTTA BE A PRODUCER,*
DRINK CHAMPAGNE UNTIL I PUKE.

CHORUS GIRLS *DRINK CHAMPAGNE 'TIL HE PUKES!*

LEO *I WANNA BE A PRODUCER,*
SHOW THE WORLD JUST WHAT I'VE GOT.
I'M GONNA PUT ON SHOWS THAT WILL ENTHRALL 'EM,

LEO AND CHORUS GIRLS *READ MY NAME IN WINCHELL'S COLUMN!*

CHORUS GIRLS *surround* LEO *and take his props away from him. He looks at them.*

LEO *I WANNA BE A PRODUCER*
'CAUSE IT'S EVERYTHING I'M NOT.

LEO *moves downstage alone as glitzy Broadway and the* CHORUS GIRLS *disappear upstage as the office set again enters with the* ACCOUNTANTS *at their desks.* LEO *sits glumly back down at his desk.*

ACCOUNTANTS *UNHAPPY . . . UNHAPPY . . . SO UNHAPPY . . .*
VERY VERY VERY VERY VERY VERY VERY VERY . . .
. . . SAD.

LEO *I WANNA BE A PRODUCER.*

MUSIC *buttons and the number ends.*

LEO *(standing and shouting)*

Hold everything! What am I doing here? Bialystock was right! There is a lot more to me than there is to me! Stop the world, I wanna get on!

MARKS *(rushing on)*

What in the hell is going on here?

(sniffing something in the air)

Do I smell the revolting stench of self-esteem?

(the ACCOUNTANTS all point at LEO)

Bloom, where do you think you're going? You already had your toilet break!

LEO I'm not going into the toilet! I'm going into show business! Mr. Marks, I got news for you: I quit! And you're right about one thing: you are a CPA—a Certified Public Asshole!

ACCOUNTANTS Yeah!

LEO *(to MARKS, handing him his cuffs and visor)*

Here's my visor . . . my Dixon Ticonderoga number two pencil . . . and my big finish!

CHORUS GIRLS *reenter to join him.*

I'M GONNA BE A PRODUCER,
SOUND THE HORN AND BEAT THE
DRUM.

CHORUS GIRLS AND ACCOUNTANTS
OOH!
DA-DA-DA,
DA-DA-DA,
DA-DA-DA,
AAH!

LEO
I'M GONNA BE A PRODUCER,
LOOK OUT BROADWAY,
HERE I COME!!

CHORUS GIRLS AND ACCOUNTANTS *(sing as LEO holds the last note, "COME")*

BROADWAY HERE HE COMES!

The CHORUS GIRLS exit on the applause as the LIGHTS begin to change, the set goes off with MARKS and the ACCOUNTANTS riding out on it, and LEO remains on stage. Scene 3 ends as Scene 4 immediately begins.

ACT ONE ▪ SCENE 4

MAX BIALYSTOCK'S *office, as in Scene 2.*

A little while later the same afternoon.

MUSIC *under: a kind of pious, church-organ version of "We Can Do It."*

MAX *is exactly where we last saw him, on his knees on the office floor, praying.* LEO *instantly appears behind him.*

LEO *(tapping* MAX *on the shoulder from behind him)*

Mr. Bialystock, I've come back. I've changed my mind.

MAX *(*MUSIC *out; jumping immediately to his feet; to God, in awe)*

Boy, you are good.

LEO Who are you talking to?

MAX Never mind. Just an old friend. What happened?

LEO *(as the* MUSIC *of "I Wanna Be a Producer" swells dramatically under)*

Just this: When I said that I could go to jail, I didn't realize that I was already in jail. I've spent my life counting other people's money. People I'm smarter than, better than. When's Leopold Bloom gonna get his share? When's it gonna be Blooms' day? I want . . . I want . . . I want . . . I want everything I've ever seen in the movies!

Our allusion to James Joyce's Ulysses. Our little inside secret in the program—this scene takes place on June 16—Bloomsday.

(P.S.—We've been amazed how many members of the audience get it every show and respond.)

MAX And, Leo, you're going to have it! 'Cause . . .

MAX *WE CAN*
DO IT, WE CAN DO IT,
SAY GOODBYE TO WOE
AND GLOOM.

LEO *I'M GONNA BE A*
PRODUCER!

MAX *WITH YOUR BRILLIANCE,*
MY RESILIENCE . . .

LEO *I'M GONNA BE A*
PRODUCER!

MAX *UP TOGETHER . . .*

MAX AND LEO *. . . WE WILL ZOOM*
WE CAN DO IT, WE CAN DO IT . . .

MAX *EV'RY SHOW I TOUCH I DOOM!*

MAX AND LEO *WE WERE FATED, TO BE MATED,*
WE'RE BIALYSTOCK AND BLOOM!

OFFSTAGE CHORUS *AAH!*

As the reprise ends to applause, a water display occurs upstage of the office. Following which, LIGHTS *slowly dim to black, and tick-tock clock* MUSIC *is briefly heard to indicate a passage of time. Meanwhile,* MAX *and* LEO *cross upstage and take off their jackets so as to be in their shirtsleeves.*

ACT ONE ▪ SCENE 5

LIGHTS *gradually up as we now discover* MAX *lying on the sofa reading from a play script while* LEO *is sitting in a nearby chair doing the same. They are surrounded by stacks of dozens of play scripts that have come in on a pallet or whatever. The intended effect is that we have gone from late afternoon of one day to dawn of the next.*

LEO Max, I can't go on. I can't read anymore. How many plays can a person read?

MAX Stop complaining! We've got to find the worst play ever written!

LEO But we've been reading all night.

MAX Who cares? You wanna be a producer? Read, read. Keep reading.

(opening a new script)

Here's one. Act One, Scene One. "Gregor Samsa awoke one morning to discover that he had been transformed into a giant cockroach."

(he thinks for a beat or two and then tosses the script aside)

Naaaa, too good.

LEO (*starting to read yet another script*)

"How could you have seen me? The glass was frosted." Wait a minute, wait a minute. I've read this play. I know I've read this play. What's the name of it? *The Frosted Glass.* I'm reading plays I read last night. I can't go on, it's too much. Max, let's face it, we'll never find it.

MAX (*sitting up with the new script he has been reading in hand*)

Ha ha ha ha ha ha ha. Ho, ho, ho. We'll never find it, eh? We'll never find it, eh? We'll never find it, eh? Leo, see it. Smell it. Touch it. Kiss it. It's the motherlode. The mother of them all.

LEO What is it? You found a flop?

MAX A flop, that's putting it mildly. This is a catastrophe. A disaster. Certain to offend peoples of all races, creeds, and religions. A guaranteed-to-close-in-one-night beauty.

LEO Let's see it.

(*taking it and reading the title page*)

Springtime for Hitler, A Gay Romp with Adolf and Eva at Berchtesgaden. Oh, my God!

MAX "Oh, my God" is right. It's practically a love letter to Hitler.

LEO It won't run a week.

MAX A week? Are you kidding?

(*pointing at the script in* LEO*'s hand*)

This play has got to close on page 4. What's the author's name again?

LEO Franz Liebkind. 61 Jane Street, New York, New York.

Originally 62 Jane Street, the address of Renée and Harry Lorayne, the world-famed memory expert who keeps forgetting that Mel Brooks is one of his best friends. Changed to 61 Jane Street, currently the address of Carolyn and Thomas Meehan, who wrote this self-serving annotation.

MAX Jane Street, Jane Street? The village, Off Broadway. I hate Off Broadway. Mimes, experimental theater, no parking. It's a jungle

down there. Let's go. We'll get the Broadway rights to *Springtime for Hitler* even if we have to go so far as to pay him.

(as he puts on his producer's Homburg hat)

C'mon.

LEO *(indicating a second producer's Homburg hanging on the hat rack)*

This other hat. May I wear it?

MAX No, you may not.

LEO Why?

MAX Because that's a Broadway producer's hat and you don't get to wear a Broadway producer's hat until you're a Broadway producer. And you're not a Broadway producer until . . .

LEO I know. Until I produce a show on Broadway. But I'm gonna wear that hat. And soon, too. 'Cause . . .

(sings to MUSIC *of "I Wanna Be a Producer")*

WE'RE GONNA BE THE PRODUCERS . . .

MAX *YES, WE'RE HEADING TO THE TOP!*

LEO AND MAX *WE'RE GONNA BE THE PRODUCERS*
OF A GREAT BIG BROADWAY FLOP!

The end of this brief reprise marks the end of Scene 5 as LIGHTS *and* SCENERY *change and we segue into Scene 6.*

ACT ONE · SCENE 6

The rooftop of a Greenwich Village apartment building on Jane Street. Later the same morning, at around ten.

In the movie, the pigeons were real. In the show, they become Franz Liebkind's chorus of back-up singers—Just one of the brilliant conceptions of our fearless leader, Susan Stroman.

FRANZ LIEBKIND, *a wild-eyed German immigrant in lederhosen and a German Army helmet, is preparing to feed his homing pigeons as he sings to himself.* MUSIC *under the song he is singing, "In Old Bavaria." There are eight Muppet-like puppet pigeons in each cage.*

FRANZ *(sings; cooing pigeons provide fills, support, and a big finish)*

OH, HOW I MISS THE HILLS AND DALES AND VALES AND TRAILS OF OLD BAVARIA.
OH, IT'S SUCH BLISS TO KISS THE MISS I MISS LIKE THIS IN OLD BAVARIA.
OH, THE MEADOWS AND THE MOUNTAINS
AND THE SKY . . .

PIGEONS *COO COO*

FRANZ *NOT TO MENTION HORDES OF*
BROWNSHIRTS PASSING BY . . .

PIGEONS *COO COO*

FRANZ *BRING A TEAR TO EVERY SINGLE NAZI EYE,*
IN OLD—I'M TALKING OLD—BA-VAR-I-A!

(as his pigeons join him in cooing to the last note—to the tune of "Über Alles"—in perfect pigeon harmony)

PIGEONS *COO COO—COO COO*
COO COO
COO COO
COO

FRANZ Very good. All right, my lieblings, chow time!

FRANZ *busies himself with his pigeons and so doesn't notice as* MAX *and* LEO *now enter the rooftop stage left.*

MAX It's just a hunch, but I'm betting this is our man.

LEO He's wearing Lederhosen and a German helmet.

MAX Don't notice it. Don't notice anything. Always look straight ahead. We need that play.

(as he and LEO *cross to* FRANZ*)*

Franz Liebkind?

FRANZ *(with a heavy German accent)*

I vas never a member of the Nazi party. I only followed orders. I had nossing to do with the war. I didn't even know there vas a war on. Ve lived in the back. Right across from Svitzerland. All ve heard vas yodeling.

(he yodels a bit to prove his point and then abruptly stops to shout)

Who are you?!

MAX Relax, Mr. Liebkind, we're not from the government. We're producers, Bialystock and Bloom. Here to talk to you about your play.

FRANZ My play? You mean *Springtime for* . . . You-Know-Who?

MAX Yes.

FRANZ Vat about it?

MAX We love it. We think it's a masterpiece.

LEO We want to put it on Broadway.

FRANZ Broadway? Oh, joy of joys. Oh, dream of dreams. I can't believe it. I must tell my birds.

MAX Tell your birds.

FRANZ Otto, Bertha, Heidi, Heinz, Volfgang . . . Adolph! Do you hear? Ve are going to clear the Führer's name! Ach, Broadvay! Lights, music, happy tippy-tappy toes. You know, not many people know it, but the Führer vas a terrific dancer.

MAX Really? We didn't know that, did we, Leo?

LEO No, we didn't.

FRANZ *(angry, more than slightly nuts)*

That's because you vere taken in by the BBC. Filthy British lies. But they never said a bad vord about Vinston Churchill, did they? Churchill! Vit his cigars, vit his brandy, and his rotten paintings! Rotten! Hitler! There vas a painter! He could paint an entire apartment in one afternoon. Two coats!

MAX Of course he could, Mr. Liebkind. And that's exactly why we want to produce your play. To show the world the true Hitler. The Hitler you loved, the Hitler you knew, the Hitler with a song in his heart.

(taking out a contract and a pen and thrusting them on FRANZ)

Here, Franz Liebkind, sign here and make your dream a reality.

FRANZ Nein.

MAX Nein?

FRANZ No.

MAX No?

FRANZ First you must prove to me that you believe as I believe. By joining vit me in singing and dancing the Führer's favorite tune . . . "Der Guten Tag Hop Clop"!

LEO "Der Guten Tag Hop Clop"?

MAX "Der Guten Tag Hop Clop."

LEO Oh, no, Mr. Liebkind, I could never sing Hitler's favorite . . . .

MAX Delighted!

(aside to LEO*)*

Shut up, he's almost ready to sign.

FRANZ Okay, here ve go. First you vill roll up your pants. Jawohl?

MAX *(he rolls up his pants legs, revealing socks with garters)*

Jawohl!

LEO *(reluctantly rolling up his pants legs to reveal skimpy ankle socks and very pale white shins)*

Jawohl.

FRANZ Good, good. Key of E . . .

MAX Is there any other?

FRANZ Vunderbar! Eins, zwei, drei . . .

FRANZ *links arms with* MAX *and* LEO *and leads them in singing "Der Guten Tag Hop Clop," a parody of a traditional Bavarian folk song.*

GUTEN TAG HOP HOP,
GUTEN TAG CLOP CLOP,
ACH DU LIEBER
UND OH BOY!
GUTEN TAG CLAP CLAP,
GUTEN TAG SLAP SLAP,
ACH DU LIEBER
VAT A JOY!

FRANZ *OH, VE ESSEN UND FRESSEN*
UND TANZEN UND TRINKEN,
TANZEN UND TRINKEN
UNTIL VE GET STINKIN'!

Everybody!

FRANZ, MAX, AND LEO *GUTEN TAG HOP HOP,*
GUTEN TAG CLOP CLOP . . .

FRANZ *GUTEN TAG*
MEIN LIEBE SCHATZ.
SO VE HOP OUR HOPS,
UND VE CLOP OUR CLOPS,
UND VE DRINK OUR SCHNAPPS
'TIL VE PLOTZ!

You vill svay!

MAX Ve vill svay.

As MUSIC *continues,* FRANZ *now leads* MAX *and* LEO *in a parody of a traditional Bavarian folk/clog dance.*

FRANZ Follow me.

MAX Very good.

At the end of each section of the dance, FRANZ *slaps* LEO *across the face and kicks him in the ass. There is a pause in the music during which an increasingly furious* LEO *wants to slap back at* FRANZ *while* MAX *restrains him.*

FRANZ Hands mach spiel.
This is a tricky one.

FRANZ cheerfully starts another section of the dance, which unfortunately for MAX and LEO ends with yet another slap and kick.

MAX Come on, it's fun! Kind of.

FRANZ Ha ha! Zee Hop Clop! Oh, it's been so long!

MAX It's sort of a Nazi hoedown.

Following the penultimate section of the dance, MUSIC continues under the following extended sequence of dialogue.

FRANZ Vunderbar! Gentlemen, I like your dancing.

MAX You're too kind.

FRANZ You may produce my play . . .

MAX Excellent!

LEO hands MAX a contract.

FRANZ . . . but only if you vill take the Siegfried Oath.

(MUSIC: Sting)

LEO The Siegfried Oath? What's that?

FRANZ A pledge of eternal allegiance to our beloved Führer!

LEO Never . . .

(MAX gives him a painful poke in the ribs)

. . . took that oath before.

FRANZ *(taking out three Nazi armbands from his pocket, hands one to each)*

Gut! Von for me, von for you, und von for you!

LEO *(looking aghast at his armband)*

Never . . .

(as MAX again pokes him in the ribs)

. . . had one on before. Thank you.

FRANZ You're velcome.

MAX Nice colors.

MAX and LEO each raise their right forefinger but then, when FRANZ isn't looking while administering the oath, they will switch to their right middle fingers.

LEO *(aside to MAX)*

We never should've started this. We're getting in too deep.

This is the first appearance of the running gag "in too deep." We got three laughs out of this one line.

MAX *(aside to LEO)*

Relax. This is nothing. I'll tell you when we're getting in too deep.

FRANZ Now, you vill raise your right forefingers und repeat after me: I solemnly svear . . .

MAX AND LEO I solemnly svear . . .

FRANZ . . . to obey the sacred Siegfried Oath . . .

MAX AND LEO . . . to obey the sacred Siegfried Oath . . .

FRANZ . . . und . . .

MAX *(switching to his middle finger)*

. . . und . . .

SIEGFRIED OATH

LEO: MAX, I CAN'T GO ON, I NEVER SHOULD HAVE STARTED THIS, ~~I'M~~ WE'RE IN ~~DEEP~~ TOO DEEP

P.1-10-64

MAX: ~~?~~ "TOO DEEP?" THIS IS NOTHING. I'LL TELL YOU WHEN ~~IT'S TOO DEEP~~. WE'RE IN TOO DEEP

When Mel came up with the name Adolf "Elizabeth" in his office in Culver City, Tom fell on the floor laughing. This was also the beginning of another running gag.

LEO *(switching to his middle finger)*

. . . und . . .

FRANZ . . . never, never, never . . .

MAX AND LEO *(flexing their fingers as they speak)*

. . . never, never, never . . .

FRANZ . . . dishonor the spirit and the memory of Adolf Elizabeth Hitler!

MAX AND LEO Dishonor the . . . Elizabeth?

FRANZ Ja. That vas his middle name. Not many people know it, but the Führer vas descended from a long line of English queens.

MAX Really?

MAX AND LEO *(together, finishing the oath)*

Adolf Elizabeth Hitler.

FRANZ Gut! So now I sign your contract.

MAX Excellent. Right on the dotted line. There you are. You'll never regret this. Thank you, Herr Liebkind.

FRANZ Jawohl!

MAX All righty then . . .

FRANZ Sehr gut!

(MAX and LEO start to leave)

HALT!

(MAX and LEO stop in their tracks)

FRANZ I forgot to tell you, the penalty for breaking the Siegried Oath is dess!

MAX Dess? Is that anything like death?

FRANZ Jawohl!

MAX Sorry to hear that. Well, we'll iron out all the details over strudel. Ta-ta.

MAX hustles LEO off as the birds coo and flutter and FRANZ waves goodbye.

FRANZ *(leaning against the door)*

Vat nice guys. Broadvay. Vait till they hear about this in Argentina! Ach, mein lieblings!

VE'RE WINKEN UND BLINKEN
UND CLINKEN UND DRINKEN
OUR SCHNAPPS
'TIL VE PLOTZ!

(he clasps his hands over his heart, and the pigeons, now each wearing a Nazi armband, make the Nazi salute)

Heil You-Know-Who!

The number comes to a finish and applause. The LIGHTS and the SCENERY begin to change as the scene ends and we segue into Scene 7.

ACT ONE ▪ SCENE 7

The elegant front foyer and large living room of ROGER DE BRIS*'s Upper East Side townhouse.*

Later the same day.

The MUSIC *of "Keep It Gay" plays the scene on and then goes out as we hear the* SOUND *of a telephone ringing on the empty stage. After a beat or two,* CARMEN GHIA*, a thin, strange-looking man in a black turtleneck sweater, enters and, as* MUSIC *goes out, answers the phone.*

Maybe only we are amused that this is also the exact description of Act One, Scene 7, that we put in the PLAYBILL for the show.

CARMEN Hello. The living room of renowned theatrical director Roger De Bris's elegant Upper East Side townhouse on a sunny Tuesday afternoon in June. Whom shall I say is calling? . . . Listen, you broken-down old queen, he was drunk, he was hot, you got lucky. Don't ever call here again!

(He angrily hangs up)

ROGER *(calling from off-stage left)*

Who was that?

CARMEN *(calling back to him)*

Wrong number!

A doorbell CHIMES *the identifying notes of "I Feel Pretty" in the foyer, stage right, and he crosses to answer the door, which he opens to reveal* MAX *and* LEO *on the doorstep, still wearing the Nazi armbands.*

Yesssssssss . . .

MAX *and* LEO *exchange looks as the hiss on the end of his "yes" goes on seemingly forever.*

. . . sssssssss.

MAX Hello. I am Max Bialystock and this is my associate, Mr. Bloom. We have an appointment with renowned theatrical director Roger De Bris.

CARMEN Ah, yes. Please, come in, please.

MAX *(as* MAX *and* LEO *enter)*

Thank you.

CARMEN How do you do? I'm Carmen Ghia. Mr. De Bris's common-law assistant. You are expected. May I take your hat, your coat, and your swastikas?

MAX Oh, these, ha, ha, just a little joke. Hope you enjoyed it.

(aside to LEO*, as* CARMEN *takes* MAX*'s hat,* LEO*'s coat, and the armbands and places them on a coatrack)*

Why didn't you tell me we still had these on?

LEO *(aside to* MAX*)*

I didn't notice them. You told me to look straight ahead. Do you remember that?

A tip of the Brooksian hat to not only The Producers movie but also to Marty Feldman in Young Frankenstein.

MAX All right, let's not fight.

CARMEN Walk this way, pleasssse.

CARMEN *minces back into the living room.* MAX *and* LEO *follow behind, mimicking the way he walks.*

CARMEN Roger! We are not alone.

He exits up the stairs.

LEO This Roger De Bris, is he good? I mean, is he bad?

MAX He stinks. That's why we're here. This guy couldn't direct you to the bathroom.

CARMEN *(entering)*

Here's Roger!

ROGER DE BRIS *(enters, descends the stairs. He is in a silvery, full-length Art Deco gown)*

Ahhh, Messrs. Bialystock and Bloom, I presume. Forgive the pun.

MAX Ha, ha, ha, ha, ha.

LEO *(aside to* MAX*)*

What pun?

MAX *(aside to* LEO*)*

Shut up. He thinks he's witty. Ah, Roger, good to see you again.

LEO *(aside to* MAX*)*

Max, he's wearing a dress.

MAX *(aside to* LEO*)*

No kidding.

(to ROGER*)*

Roger, you look gorgeous. Gorgeous.

ROGER Merci. Oh, by the way, Max, darling, we loved *Funny Boy*, didn't we, Carmen?

CARMEN Worshiped it!

TO BE OR NOT TO BE . . .

CARMEN AND ROGER . . . *YOU MEAN A LOT TO ME . . . .*

ROGER Showstopper!

CARMEN Fabulous!

ROGER Oh, dear, your Mr. Bloom is staring at my gown.

LEO Oh, well, I . . .

ROGER I should explain. I'm going to the Choreographer's Ball this evening. There is a prize for best costume.

CARMEN We always win.

ROGER *(looking in a mirror as he puts on a pointed Art Deco tiara; turning back to face front)*

I'm not so sure about this year. I'm supposed to be the Grand Duchess Anastasia. But I think I look more like the Chrysler Building.

CARMEN As far as I'm concerned, without your wig on, you're only half-dressed.

ROGER Well, then, why don't you go and get it, oh Wicked Witch of the West?

CARMEN If your intention was to shoot an arrow through my heart . . . bull's-eye!

(he exits)

ROGER What do you think of my gown, Mr. Bloom? Be brutal, brutal. God knows they will.

LEO Uh . . . where do you keep your wallet?

MAX What a kidder. Roger, let's face it, that building is you. Listen, I know we sent it to you only this morning, but did you get a chance yet to read *Springtime for Hitler*?

ROGER Read it? I devoured it! And I found it remarkable, remarkable. I feel that it is a very important piece. Drenched with historical goodies. I for one, for instance, never realized that the Third Reich meant Germany.

MAX Yeah, how about that? Then you'll do it?

ROGER Do it? Of course not. Not my kind of thing. I mean, Max, please, World War Two? Too dark, too depressing . . . .

(sings, as CARMEN *reenters)*

THE THEATER'S SO OBSESSED
WITH DRAMAS SO DEPRESSED,
IT'S HARD TO SELL A TICKET ON BROADWAY.
SHOWS SHOULD BE MORE PRETTY,
SHOWS SHOULD BE MORE WITTY,
SHOWS SHOULD BE MORE . . .

What's the word?

LEO Gay?

ROGER Exactly!

NO MATTER WHAT YOU DO ON THE STAGE
KEEP IT LIGHT, KEEP IT BRIGHT, KEEP IT GAY!
WHETHER IT'S MURDER, MAYHEM, OR RAGE.
DON'T COMPLAIN, IT'S A PAIN, KEEP IT GAY!

CARMEN *PEOPLE WANT LAUGHTER WHEN THEY SEE A SHOW,*
THE LAST THING THEY'RE AFTER'S
A LITANY OF WOE.

ROGER AND CARMEN *A HAPPY ENDING WILL PEP UP YOUR PLAY . . .*

ROGER *OEDIPUS WON'T BOMB . . .*

CARMEN *. . . IF HE WINDS UP WITH MOM!*

ROGER *KEEP IT GAY . . .*

CARMEN *KEEP IT GAY . . .*

ROGER AND CARMEN *KEEP IT GAY!*

MAX Couldn't agree with you more. And you have our blessings, Roger, to make *Springtime for Hitler* just as gay as anyone could possibly want. So, c'mon, do it for us, please.

ROGER *(speaks as* MUSIC *continues under)*

No, I'm sorry, Max, but it's simply not my cup of tea. Still, fair is fair, perhaps I should ask my production team what they think.

MAX Your production team? Who are they?

ROGER You'll see. They all live here.

(calling to off-stage left)

Oh, guys! Come say hello to Bialystock and Bloom!

(to MAX *and* LEO *as* MUSIC *continues;* BRYAN *enters)*

This is my set designer, Bryan.

BRYAN *KEEP IT GLAD, KEEP IT MAD, KEEP IT GAY!*

Originally, in this scene each member of the entourage was introduced as if in a fashion show.

FIX ON P. 71

(MUSIC UNDER "KEEP IT GAY" PLAYED AS A WALTZ UNDERNEATH)

ROGER
GENTLEMEN, LET ME INTRODUCE MY TEAM,
ONE BY LOVELY ONE...

AH, FIRST, WEARING A STUNNING
OFF-THE-SHOULDER BALENCIAGA,
MY CHOREOGRAPHER, BRUCE

DIOR

BRUCE

Hi!

ROGER

AND HERE, IN A SPORTING COCO CHANEL FAUX-LEATHER HIS OR HER FAUX-LIZARD THREE-BUTTON SUIT, WITH MATCHING HAT AND BAG,
MY SET DESIGNER, KEVIN.

3-BUTTON
HIS OR HER
EVENING PANTS
SUIT.

SCHIAPARELLI

KEVIN

HELLO THERE.

BIALYSTOCK
(TO BLOOM)
I WONDER IF THAT COMES WITH 2 PAIR OF PANTS?

A DEVASTATING

A CHI-CHI
GIVENCHY
BLOCKBUSTER,

MY

AND NEXT, BATHED IN A
FETCHING JAQUES FATH
FEATHERED FANTASY,
MY COSTUME DESIGNER,
SCOTT.

MAINBOCHER
DIOR
LILY DACHE
NORELL
MOLLINUX
PAULINE TRIGERE
PATOU
LANVIN
GIVENCHY

SCOTT
MY PLEASURE.

RALPH
HI, GUYS, HOW THEY HANGING?

BIALYSTOCK
OUR PLEASURE
(BLOOM SHAKES ... NO)

AND FINALLY,

ROGER *(as* KEVIN *enters)*

And here's my costume designer, Kevin.

KEVIN Hello . . .

KEEP IT HAPPY, KEEP IT SNAPPY, KEEP IT GAY!

BRYAN AND KEVIN *WE'RE CLEVER, CREATIVE,*
IT'S OUR JOB TO SEE
THAT EV'RYTHING'S PERFECT FOR MR. DE BRIS!

ROGER *(as* SCOTT *enters)*

NEXT, SCOTT, MY CHOREOGRAPHER . . .

SCOTT Hi there . . .

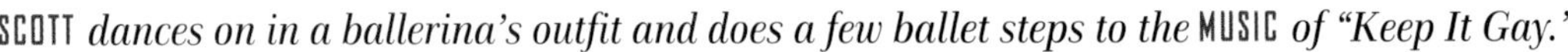

SCOTT *dances on in a ballerina's outfit and does a few ballet steps to the* MUSIC *of "Keep It Gay."*

ROGER And, ah, finally, last and least, my lighting designer, Shirley Markowitz.

SHIRLEY *(a squat fireplug of a woman; sings in a low masculine voice as she enters)*

KEEP IT GAY, KEEP IT GAY, KEEP IT GAY.

ROGER *(as* MUSIC *continues under)*

They've all just read *Springtime.* What do you think of it, fellas?

KEVIN It needs sequins.

BRYAN It needs glamour.

SCOTT It needs glitz.

SHIRLEY It needs tits.

MAX *(aside to* LEO*)*

We're losin' them. Go say something nice to Roger. I think he likes you.

IDEA –

BUILD ON "KEEP IT GAY" CHORUSES

KEEP IT BRIGHT

" " LIGHT

KEEP IT UP

UP-TEMPO

UP-BEAT

LEO *(aside to* MAX*)*

But Max . . .

MAX *(pushing* LEO *toward* ROGER*)*

Go on, it's just showbiz . . .

LEO Uh, Mr. De Bris, Roger, I think your gown is actually very stunning.

ROGER Why thank you, Mr. Bloom, Leo. Umm, what is that enchanting cologne you're wearing?

LEO Me? I'm not wearing any cologne.

ROGER You mean that smell is you? God, if I could bottle you, I'd shove you under my armpits every day.

LEO *(involuntarily gasping)*

Aaaahhh.

*(*LEO *hugs* MAX*)*

Max, we never should have started this. We're getting in too deep.

MAX *(aside to* LEO*)*

Too deep, this is nothing, I'll tell you when we're getting in too deep.

CARMEN *AND SO THE RULE IS WHEN "MOUNTING" A PLAY . . .*

ROGER, CARMEN, AND TEAM *KEEP IT FUNNY, KEEP IT SUNNY, KEEP IT GAY!*

ROGER, CARMEN, AND TEAM *(hum "Keep It Gay" as* CARMEN *arranges wig on* ROGER. MUSIC *continues under tremolo during the following sequence of dialogue)*

LEO *(aside to* MAX*)*

I don't think we're getting to them. What do we do now?

MAX *(aside to* LEO*)*

Watch this.

(going to ROGER*)*

Roger, listen, I think that *Springtime for Hitler* would be a marvelous opportunity for you. I mean, up to now, you've always been associated with frivolous musicals.

ROGER You're right. I've often felt as though I've been throwing my life away on silly entertainments. Dopey showgirls in gooey gowns. Two-three-kick-turn! Turn-turn-kick-turn!

CARMEN Oh, Roger.

ROGER It's enough to make you heave. Nonetheless, sorry, Max, I just couldn't do *Springtime for Hitler.*

MAX Why not? Think of the prestige.

ROGER No.

MAX Think of the respect.

ROGER No, no, no.

MAX Think of . . . the Tony!

CARMEN AND THE TEAM *(sing as* ROGER *is suddenly interested at the thought of winning a Tony)*

TONY . . . TONY . . . TONY . . . TONY . . . TONY!

ROGER (*struck by a vision, yells*)

Ngaaaahhhhh!

MAX What's the matter?

LEO Is he all right?

CARMEN He's having a stroke . . .

MAX AND LEO What?

CARMEN . . . of genius!

ROGER I see it! I see it! At last the chance to do something important!

CARMEN *ROGER DE BRIS*
PRESENTS HISTORY!

ROGER Of course, that whole second act has to be rewritten. They're losing the war? Excuse me. It's too downbeat.

CARMEN *ROGER DE BRIS PRESENTS HISTORY!*

ROGER But maybe . . . it's a wild idea, but it just might work . . .

I SEE A LINE OF BEAUTIFUL GIRLS
DRESSED AS STORM TROOPERS, EACH ONE A GEM,
WITH LEATHER BOOTS AND WHIPS ON THEIR HIPS,
IT'S RISQUÉ, DARE I SAY, S AND M!

CARMEN AND THE TEAM Love it!

ROGER *I SEE GERMAN SOLDIERS DANCING THROUGH FRANCE,*
PLAYED BY CHORUS BOYS IN VERY TIGHT PANTS.
AND WAIT, THERE'S MORE—THEY WIN THE WAR!

AND THE DANCES THEY DO WILL BE DARING AND NEW,
TURN-TURN-KICK-TURN, TURN-TURN-KICK-TURN,
ONE-TWO-THREE, KICK-TURN!
KEEP IT SASSY, KEEP IT CLASSY, KEEP IT . . .

MAX That is brilliant. Brilliant! Roger, I speak for Mr. Bloom and myself, when I say that you are the only man in the world who can do justice to *Springtime for Hitler.* Will you do it, please?

LEO Please.

ROGER Wait a minute. This is a very big decision. It might affect the course of my entire life. I shall have to think about it . . . I'll do it.

MAX *and* LEO *happily shake hands as the* MUSIC *of "Keep It Gay" instantly again strikes up.*

I'LL DO IT!

Sabu, champagne!

A dark-skinned HOUSEBOY *enters, serves glasses of champagne, and joins the number. In a turban, bare-chested and barefoot, wearing only a loincloth, he looks like Sabu.*

CARMEN AND THE TEAM *(gasp)*

Ah!

ROGER, CARMEN, AND THE TEAM *IF AT THE END YOU WANT THEM TO CHEER . . .*
KEEP IT GAY, KEEP IT GAY, KEEP IT GAY.
WHETHER IT'S HAMLET, OTHELLO, OR LEAR . . .
KEEP IT GAY, KEEP IT GAY, KEEP IT GAY.

CARMEN *COMEDY'S JOYOUS, A CONSTANT DELIGHT,*
DRAMAS ANNOY US . . .

ROGER AND CARMEN *. . . AND RUIN OUR NIGHT.*

ROGER, CARMEN, AND THE TEAM *SO KEEP YOUR STRINDBERGS AND IBSENS AT BAY . . .*

ROGER *(sings as* MAX *thrusts a contract in front of him)*

I'LL SIGN . . .

KEVIN *SIGN . . .*

BRYAN *SIGN . . .*

Lost in one of his earlier drafts was one of Mel's cleverest bits of lyric writing, in which he slipped in both the first and last name of one of Russia's greatest writers on two different lines: "Oscar Wilde should be your maxim, Gorki's gonna tax 'em, keep it gay, keep it gay, keep it gay!"

SCOTT *SIGN . . .*

CARMEN *SIGN . . .*

SHIRLEY *SIGN . . .*

MAX AND LEO Sign . . .

ROGER Roger Elizabeth De Bris!

ALL *KEEP IT GAY!!!*

MAX AND LEO *GAY!!!*

ALL *LA LA LA LA LA LA LA LA LA,*
KEEP IT GAY, KEEP IT GAY,
KEEP IT GAY!
LA LA LA LA LA LA LA LA LA,
KEEP IT . . .

ROGER Conga!

ALL *LA LA LA LA LA LA LA LA LA*
LA LA LA LA,
LA LA LA LA LA LA LA LA LA
LA LA,
AND SO THE RULE IS WHEN
MOUNTING A PLAY,
KEEP IT GAY, KEEP IT GAY,
KEEP IT GAY!

The number comes to a huge finish as LIGHTS *change,* SCENERY *begins to move, and Scene 7 ends as we segue into . . .*

ACT ONE – SCENE 8

The office.

Later the same afternoon. The MUSIC *of "When You Got, Flaunt It!" plays the scene on and then goes out as* MAX *and* LEO *enter.* MAX *is ebullient.* LEO *is still in a daze after his experience with* ROGER *et al.*

MAX *(as he enters, waving a pair of signed contracts)*

Exclusive Broadway rights to the worst show ever written! And a signed contract with the worst director who ever lived! We're in business!

LEO And what a business. In the same day I'm taking the Siegfried Oath and dancing the conga with a sailor, a cop, and an extremely friendly Cherokee Indian.

MAX When he said, "Let's smoke-um peace pipe," I knew it was time to go. It's not easy being a Broadway producer.

(putting his arm around LEO*'s shoulders)*

But together we'll make it, partners, Leo, all the way, and nothing, or no one, will ever come between us.

LEO Right, Max, nothing, or no one.

They shake hands as there is a knock on the office door.

LEO AND MAX Come in!

ULLA, *a gorgeous young Swedish blonde, clearly a knockout, wearing a white raincoat, enters and stands in the doorway.* MUSIC*: Sting.*

ULLA *(with a Swedish accent)*

Bialystock 'n' Bloom? Gut tag pa dig.

LEO What?

ULLA Oh, excuse me. Ay bane Svenska–Svedish. Casting today?

LEO Oh, sorry, miss, no, we won't be casting for at least another few . . .

MAX *(hastily interrupting* LEO*)*

Casting! Casting! Yes, we just started casting today!

LEO We're casting?

MAX We're casting.

(quietly aside to LEO*)*

If you don't mind, just once in my life I'd like to see somebody on that couch who's under eighty-five.

(to ULLA*)*

What's your name, my dear?

ULLA My name is Ulla Inga Hansen Bensen Yonsen Tallen-Hallen Svaden-Svanson.

MAX Wait! What's your first name?

ULLA That vas my first name. You vanna hear my last name?

MAX We don't have the time. We'll call you Ulla. What do you do, Ulla?

ULLA Ulla sing and dance. You vant Ulla make audition?

LEO No, no, miss, that won't be . . .

MAX Yes, make audition, make audition. Make audition all over the office.

LEO All right, make audition.

ULLA Picture. Résumé.

LEO What are you going to sing?

ULLA Vell, yesterday, ven I vas stepping out of a big white Rolls Royce limo, a crazy person yelled something out a vindow that inspired me to write this song.

In the movie, Ulla opens her coat and is wearing a bikini, which we knew would be wrong for Broadway. In the musical, we wanted a more real, sympathetic love interest for Leo Bloom.

As she begins the song, ULLA *removes her raincoat to reveal that she is wearing a very short tight-fitting dress.*

WHEN ~~IF~~ YOU GOT IT, FLAUNT IT,

STEP RIGHT OUT AND STRUT YOUR STUFF

(1) ~~SHOW THE WORLD JUST WHAT YOU'VE GOT~~

ULLA (CONT'D) *(sings, with a Swedish accent)*

VEN YOU GOT IT, FLAUNT IT,
STEP RIGHT UP AND STRUT YOUR STUFF.
PEOPLE TELL YOU MODESTY'S A WIRTUE,
BUT IN THE THEATER MODESTY CAN HURT YOU.

VEN YOU GOT IT, FLAUNT IT,
SHOW YOUR ASSETS, LET 'EM KNOW YOU'RE PROUD.

YOUR GOODIES YOU MUST PUSH,
STICK YOUR CHEST OUT, SHAKE YOUR TUSH,
VEN YOU GOT IT, SHOUT IT OUT LOUD!

Now Ulla dance.

(a dance section, after which she again sings)

VEN YOU GOT IT, SHOW IT,
PUT YOUR HIDDEN TREASURES ON DISPLAY.
VIOLINISTS LOVE TO PLAY AN E-STRING,
BUT AUDIENCES REALLY LOVE A G-STRING.
VEN YOU GOT IT, SHOUT IT,
LET THE WHOLE VORLD HEAR VAT YOU'RE ABOUT.
CLOTHES MAY MAKE THE MAN,
ALL A GIRL NEEDS IS A TAN.
VEN YOU GOT IT, LET IT HANG OUT!

Remember ven Ulla dance?

MAX AND LEO Yeah!

ULLA Ulla dance again!

(a second dance section, and she again sings)

VEN I WAS YUST A LITTLE GIRL IN SVEDEN
MY THOUGHTFUL MOTHER GAVE ME THIS ADVICE:
IF NATURE BLESSES YOU FROM TOP TO BOTTOM,
SHOW THAT TOP TO BOTTOM, DON'T THINK TWICE . . .

Now Ulla belt!

DON'T THINK TWICE . . . !

VEN YOU GOT IT, SHARE IT,
LET THE PUBLIC FEAST UPON YOUR CHARMS,
PEOPLE SAY THAT BEING PRIM IS PROPER,
BUT EV'RY SHOWGIRL KNOWS THAT PRIM WILL STOP HER.
VEN YOU GOT IT, GIVE IT,
DON'T BE SELFISH, GIVE IT ALL A-VAY.
DON'T BE SHY, BE BOLD 'N' CUTE,
SHOW THE BOYS THAT BIRTHDAY SUIT.
VEN YOU GOT IT, IF YOU GOT IT,
ONCE YOU GOT IT, SHOUT OUT HOORAY!!!

(to MAX *and* LEO*, very demurely)*

Okey-dokey. You like it?

MAX Like it? I want you to know, my dear, that even though we're sitting down, we're giving you a standing ovation.

(to LEO*)*

She's in the show.

We want you to know, dear readers, that we are both very ashamed and very proud of this joke.

ULLA *(squeals)*

Ooh! Ooh! Ooh!

LEO Huh? Max, what are you talking about? There may not be a part for her in the show.

MAX Would you excuse us for a moment, my dear? Nonsense, Bloom. Do I have to teach you everything? There is always a part in the show for the producer's girlfriend.

LEO But, Max, we don't even know when we're starting rehearsals yet.

MAX So what? We're producers, aren't we? So, until she goes into the show, she can work for us here. Because, we need—nay deserve—to have ourselves a gorgeous Swedish secretary-slash-receptionist.

LEO A secretary who doesn't speak English? What will people say?

MAX They'll say, "Oooh wee-woo-woo, wah-wah-wah whoa." That's what they'll say. Offer her the job.

LEO *(to* MAX*)*

All right, if you say so.

(to ULLA*, who has started to leave)*

Wait a moment, miss, we might have a position for you.

MAX As a matter of fact, we might have several positions for you.

LEO Until the show is ready to go, we can offer you a job as a secretary-slash-receptionist.

ULLA Secretary-slash-receptionist? Okey-slash-dokey. Ay can do that.

(crosses to desk, picking up the phone)

Answer telephone. Bialystock and Bloom, Bialystock and Bloom.

MAX *(aside to* LEO*)*

Smart as a whip.

(to ULLA*)*

You're hired!

ULLA *(squeals)*

Ooh!

LEO If he says so. Secretary-slash-receptionist, and maybe you could also tidy up a little bit around here.

ULLA Tidy up? Tidy up? Such a funny word. What means tidy up?

LEO Uh, you know, clean . . .

MAX Make look nice.

ULLA Oh, ja, Ulla can make tidy up.

LEO Fine. What time can you get here in the morning?

BY THE WAY, HOW R YOUR SECRETARY SKILLS?

I CAN DO 13 WORDS A MINUTE.

13 WORDS A MINUTE, THAT'S VERY SLOW TYPING

THAT'S NOT TYPING, THAT'S TALKING.

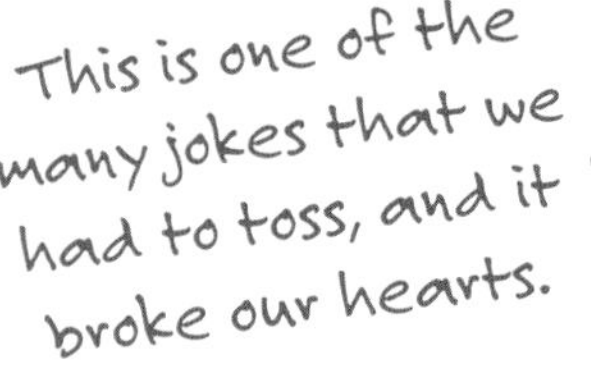

This is one of the many jokes that we had to toss, and it broke our hearts.

ULLA Vell . . . Ulla vake up every morning five a.m. From five to seven, Ulla like to exercise. From seven to eight, Ulla like to take long shower. From eight to nine, Ulla like to have big Svedish breakfast, many different herrings. From nine to eleven, Ulla like to practice her singing and her dancing. And at eleven Ulla like to have sex. What time should I get here?

MAX AND LEO Eleven!

ULLA Gut. Ulla come at eleven. Gut tag pa dig.

MAX Gut ta pa dig.

ULLA Gut ta pa dig.

MAX Gut tag pa dig.

ULLA God bless America!

(she exits)

MAX God bless Sweden.

Oy, Ulla's daily routine from rising at five a.m. until eleven a.m. We probably spent more time writing and rewriting this little routine than it took us to write the entire rest of the scene. Oh, the hours spent listing her various morning exercises, the twenty-one different kinds of herring she had for breakfast, etc., etc. Writers of the world take heed: less is definitely more.

LEO She's fantastic! The most beautiful girl I've ever seen. I've never felt this way before. It's like there's a volcano erupting deep inside of me. Hot lava rising higher and higher. What is it Max, what is it?

MAX Didn't your father ever have this talk with you?

(LEO looks forlorn)

Well, maybe when you're a little older. C'mere, I wanna show you something.

(crossing to a large safe on the floor at stage right, opening it to reveal that it is totally empty)

What do you see?

LEO Nothing.

MAX Exactly. But now that we've got our sure-fire flop, it's gonna be our job to fill that safe with two million dollars.

LEO Two million. Gee. How much do we put in?

MAX *(pretends to fall)*

How much do we put in? Bloom, the two cardinal rules of being a Broadway producer are, one, never put your own money in the show.

Tom suggested the cardinal rule be "Never put your own money in the show," and Mel said, "What about the second rule?" Tom asked, "What rule?" and Mel yelled, "NEVER put your own money in the show!"

LEO And two?

MAX *(up close in LEO's face, shouting)*

NEVER put your own money in the show! Get it?

LEO Got it.

MAX Good.

LEO So how do we get the money?

MAX How? I'll tell you how.

(he crosses and opens the cabinet with all of his pictures of little old ladies)

From my investors.

(the MUSIC *of "Along Came Bialy" played as a tango begins under)*

Hundreds of little old ladies, all looking to Max Bialystock for one last thrill. So, in days to come, Bloom, you'll see very little of me . . .

(leading LEO *to the door)*

. . . and right now I'd like to see very little of you. Scram while I get myself ready, for Max Bialystock is about to launch himself into Little Old Lady Land.

LEO *exits as* MAX *busies himself getting ready for the Little Old Ladies—pomading his hair, gargling with Listerine, putting a flower in the lapel of his jacket.*

MAX *THE TIME HAS COME*
TO BE A LOVER FROM THE ARGENTINE,
TO SLICK MY HAIR DOWN WITH BRILLIANTINE,
AND GARGLE HEAVILY WITH LISTERINE.

Wow!

IT'S TIME FOR MAX
TO PUT HIS BACKERS ON THEIR BACKS,
AND THRILL THEM WITH AMAZING ACTS,
THOSE AGING NYMPHOMANIACS . . .

(he now lets out two Tarzan-like yells similar to the sounds in Sergio Leone spaghetti westerns)

AH-AH-AH!
AH-AH-AH!

(sings as he continues to dude himself up for the Little Old Ladies)

THEY WERE HELPLESS,
THEY WERE HOPELESS,
THEN ALONG CAME BIALY!

THEY WERE JOYLESS,
THEY WERE BOYLESS,
THEN ALONG CAME BIALY!

THEY'RE MY ANGELS,
I'M THEIR DEVIL,
AND I KEEP THOSE EMBERS AGLOW!
WHEN I WOOS 'EM
I CAN'T LOSE 'EM,
'CAUSE I CAST MY SPELL 'N'
THEY START YELLIN' . . .

(shouts)

Fire down below!

Now, ready to head off to Little Old Lady Land, MAX *moves downstage as a scrim comes in behind and he continues singing alone downstage.*

MAX	*THEY WERE LISTING,* *THEY WERE SINKING,* *THEN ALONG CAME BIALY!* *THEY WERE DESP'RATE,* *THEY WERE DRINKING . . .* *THEN ALONG CAME BIALY!* *SO ROMANTIC,* *THEY WERE FRANTIC* *THEN THEIR PRAYERS* *WERE HEARD UP ABOVE*		
	HEAVEN SENT THEM	ENSEMBLE	*AAH!*
	THEIR BIALY!		*AAH!*
	I'M THE CELEBRATION *OF LOVE!*		*HE'S THE CELEBRATION* *OF LOVE!*

ACT ONE - SCENE 9

The scrim behind MAX *now rises to reveal, as a sign indicates, "Little Old Lady Land"—an abstract kind of idyllic park looking like an ornate, old-fashioned, lacy valentine. Little Old Lady Land is filled with* LITTLE OLD LADIES.

LITTLE OLD LADIES *WE WERE HELPLESS,*
WE WERE HOPELESS,
THEN ALONG CAME BIALY!

A trio of LITTLE OLD LADIES *is revealed sitting next to each other on a park bench, knitting. Each is bespectacled, white-haired, elderly, in a calf-length black dress with white-lace collar—a quintessential sweet old American grandma straight out of Norman Rockwell. A* POLICEMAN *walks by.*

LICK ME—BITE ME How-de-do?

HOLD ME—TOUCH ME *LIFE HAD PASSED US BY,*
AND LOVE HAD STOLEN AWAY.

LICK ME—BITE ME *AT THE END OF OUR ROPE*
WE'D GIVEN UP HOPE . . .
OF ONE LAST ROLL IN THE HAY.

KISS ME—FEEL ME *DISCARDED DOLLS,*
ABANDONED WRECKS.

ALL THREE LITTLE OLD LADIES *CONDEMNED TO A LIFE*
OF SITTING AND KNITTING
WHEN ALL WE REALLY WANTED WAS . . . SEX!

LIGHTS *change and then we find* MAX *sitting on a bench with a* LITTLE OLD LADY *as* PASSERS-BY *pass by behind them on a park path.*

MAX Ah, did you bring the checkee, my little turtledove?

HOLD ME—TOUCH ME *(handing him the check, which he quickly pockets)*

Yes, but first, Bialy, can we play one dirty little game?

MAX What, here in broad daylight?

HOLD ME–TOUCH ME It'll just be a quickie.

MAX Okay, what, what?

HOLD ME–TOUCH ME Let's play "The Hairless Chihuahua and the Well-Hung Great Dane."

Once upon a time, as can be heard on the CD of the show, "The Distracted Tourist and the Ever-Watchful Orangutan." We also tried "The Nervous Librarian and the Very Long Shoreman."

MAX Are you on some kind of medication? You're killing me! I'm exhausted. Please, let's play one game with absolutely no sex.

HOLD ME–TOUCH ME What?

MAX Let's play the Jewish Princess and her husband.

(MAX and HOLD ME–TOUCH ME exit off-stage left)

LITTLE OLD LADIES *SO ROMANTIC,*
WE WERE FRANTIC,
THEN OUR PRAYERS WERE HEARD UP ABOVE.
HEAVEN SENT US OUR BIALY,
HE'S THE CELEBRATION OF LOVE!

Swings appear in Little Old Lady Land. We see MAX pushing LICK ME–BITE ME on a swing.

LICK ME–BITE ME Oh, Bialy, higher!

MAX Okay.

LICK ME–BITE ME Push me higher!

MAX All right.

LICK ME–BITE ME *(handing him a check)*

Very high!

MAX Here we go!

He pushes her, and she and the swing disappear into the wings. We hear a blood-curdling scream from off-stage. The swing returns without her.

MAX *(shouting off-stage left)*

Omigod . . . you forgot to sign the check!

Originally this number dragged on and on . . .

LITTLE OLD LADY #1

I ALWAYS THOUGHT
THAT MAKING LOVE
SHOULD HAPPEN IN THE DARK,
I NEVER DREAMED
THAT MAKING LOVE
COULD EVER BE A LARK.
I WAS PAINFULLY SHY, BY GOLLY,
UNTIL I MET BIALY,
NOW WE'RE DOING IT IN BROAD
DAYLIGHT IN THE PARK.

LITTLE OLD LADY #2

I ALWAYS THOUGHT
THAT MAKING LOVE
SHOULD HAPPEN ONCE A YEAR,
I ALWAYS SAID THAT
MORE THAN THAT
WAS IN BAD TASTE, I FEAR.
I LIVED HAPPILY
WITH THIS FOLLY,
UNTIL I MET BIALY,
NOW WE'RE HITTING
THE HAY SIX TIMES
A DAY, MY DEAR.

LITTLE OLD LADY #3

I ALWAYS THOUGHT
THAT MAKING LOVE
WAS NOT THE THING TO DO,
WHEN SUITORS SOUGHT
TO HAVE THEIR WAY
I'D STOP THEM AT FIRST WOO.
I WAS PRUDISHLY PRIM,
NOT JOLLY,
UNTIL I MET BIALY,
NOW I JOYOUSLY SAY
EV'RY NIGHT AND DAY,
"LET'S SCREW!"

LITTLE OLD LADY #4

I ALWAYS THOUGHT
THAT MAKING LOVE
WAS GAUCHE, I'D NEVER YIELD,
I ALWAYS VOWED
NO LIVING SOUL
WOULD PENETRATE MY SHIELD.
I WAS COLD AS
CHRISTMAS HOLLY,
UNTIL I MET BIALY,
NOW I'M HAPPILY HUMPING
LIKE A RABBIT
IN THE FIELD.

Now, a dozen LITTLE OLD LADIES *enter, pushing walkers. There follows a tap section with the walkers providing the tap sound. At the end of the tap section, the* LITTLE OLD LADIES *scream as* MAX *re-enters.*

LITTLE OLD LADIES Max!

LITTLE OLD LADY WITH WHEELED WALKER Max!

MAX *joins in the number as he collects checks from one and all.*

MAX "Fire down below!"

LITTLE OLD LADIES *(singing and dancing while also doing all sorts of acrobatics all over the stage, including jumping on hidden trampolines upstage behind the park's hedges and bushes and thus seeming to fly through the air)*

WE WERE LISTING,
WE WERE SINKING,
THEN ALONG CAME BIALY!

WE WERE DESP'RATE,
WE WERE DRINKING,
THEN ALONG CAME BIALY!

SO ROMANTIC,
WE WERE FRANTIC
THEN OUR PRAYERS WERE HEARD
UP ABOVE!

IT'S BIALY,
HAIL, BIALY!
HE'S THE CULMINATION,
THE RESTORATION,
THE CONSUMMATION,
THE TITILLATION, MAX *EJACULATION, OY!*
HE'S THE CELEBRATION OF LOVE . . .

Now, just as "Along Came Bialy" is about to reach an orgasmic musical finish, the final note is suspended and applause is ducked as fast, pulsing MUSIC *plays under the following sequence of dialogue. As* LIGHTS *go down upstage on the* LITTLE OLD LADIES, *who freeze in place,* MAX *steps to downstage center waving the checks.*

MAX *(shouting toward the wings)*

Bloom . . . Bloom!

LEO *(as he enters and hurries up to* MAX*)*

What, Max, what?

MAX I've done it! I've done it! Look, we got the money. Now all we have to do is put on the biggest flop in history!

LEO *THAT'S GREAT!*

MAX AND LEO *(as* MUSIC *segues into "We Can Do It")*

WE CAN DO IT, WE CAN DO IT,
WE CAN MAKE A MILLION BUCKS!

ULLA *(appearing suddenly in a spotlight and pantomiming being on the phone; sings)*

BIALYSTOCK AND BLOOM, BIALYSTOCK AND BLOOM!
HE RAISED THE MONEY, BIALYSTOCK AND BLOOM,
BIALYSTOCK AND BLOOM, THE SHOW'S A GO!

LITTLE

LADY LAND

ROGER, CARMEN, *and* THE TEAM *now suddenly appear in a spotlight and join* ULLA, FRANZ, *and* MAX *and* LEO *in simultaneously singing four separate parts in a manner similar to the quintet at the end of Act One of* West Side Story.

Part 1:

ROGER AND CARMEN *HE'S RAISED THE MONEY, WE'RE ON OUR WAY,*
KEEP IT GAY, KEEP IT GAY, KEEP IT GAY!

WE HAVE OUR BACKING, OH, WHAT A DAY,
KEEP IT GAY, KEEP IT GAY, KEEP IT GAY!

WONDER OF WONDERS, WE HAVE ALL OUR CASH,
BARRING ALL BLUNDERS, WE SHOULD HAVE A SMASH!

WE KNOW THAT . . . WE CAN DO IT!

ROGER, CARMEN, AND THE TEAM *GAY, GAY, GAY, GAY . . .*
GAY, GAY, GAY, GAY . . .
GAY, GAY, GAY, GAY . . .

Part 2:

MAX AND LEO *WE CAN DO IT! WE CAN DO IT!*

WE CAN DO IT,
IT'LL BE LIKE SHOOTING DUCKS!

E'VRYTHING WE'VE EVER WANTED
IS SET TO COME OUR WAY!

WE KNOW THAT . . . WE CAN DO IT!

WE CAN MAKE IT, WE WON'T FAKE IT,
WE WERE FATED TO BE MATED . . .

Part 3:

ULLA *BIALYSTOCK AND BLOOM . . .*
BIALYSTOCK AND BLOOM . . .
BIALYSTOCK AND BLOOM!
AND BLOOM!

BIALYSTOCK AND BLOOM!
AND BLOOM!

BIALYSTOCK AND BLOOM . . .

During the finale, Kathy Fitzgerald as Shirley Markowitz flirts brazenly with Ulla. Kathy came up with that spin for the finale.

Part 4:

FRANZ *DEUTSCHLAND, DEUTSCHLAND,*
ÜBER ALLES,
ALLES IN DER WELT!

DEUTSCHLAND, DEUTSCHLAND,
ÜBER ALLES,
ALLES IN DER WELT!

Part 5:

LITTLE OLD LADIES *THEN ALONG CAME BIALY!*
WE WERE DESPERATE
WE WERE DRINKING
THEN ALONG CAME BIALY!

BIALY WAS ROMANTIC,
OUR PULSE BECAME
SO FRANTIC.

IT'S BIALY!
HAIL BIALY!
AHH!

ULLA AND FRANZ *BIALYSTOCK AND BLOOM . . .*

ULLA, FRANZ, ROGER, CARMEN, AND THE TEAM *BIALYSTOCK AND BLOOM . . .*

MAX, LEO, ULLA, FRANZ, ROGER, CARMEN, AND THE TEAM *(ending the five-part section)*
BIALYSTOCK AND BLOOM!!

Now, a huge scenery piece, a lighted sign on the roof of the Shubert Theatre, comes in from above, lighting up to say "Bialystock and Bloom Present . . . 'Springtime for Hitler,' A New Neo-Nazi Musical, Opening Soon!" The signature MUSIC *of "Springtime for Hitler" plays under.*

ALL EXCEPT MAX AND LEO *(sing to "Springtime for Hitler")*

AH-AH, AH, AH-AH
AH, AH-AH-AAH!

ALL *(sing to "Springtime for Hitler")*

AH-AH, AH, AH-AH AH, AAH!

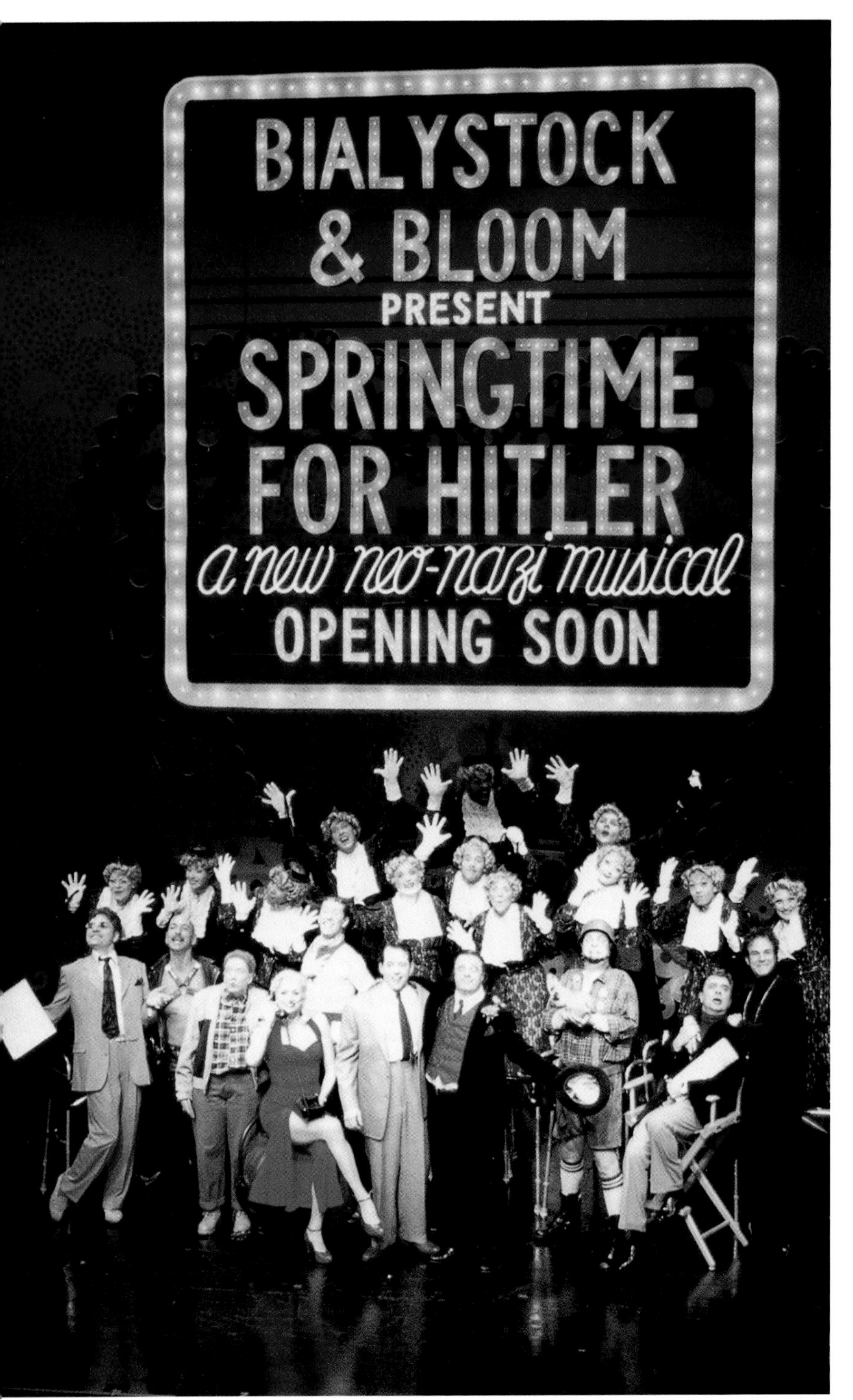

MAX AND LEO *WE CAN DO IT . . .*

ALL EXCEPT MAX AND LEO *THEY CAN DO IT . . .*

ALL *SAY GOODBYE TO WOE*
AND GLOOM.

MAX AND LEO *WE CAN DO IT . . .*

ALL EXCEPT MAX AND LEO *NOTHING TO IT . . .*

ALL *CAN'T YOU HEAR THAT*
BING-BANG-BOOM!!

ALL EXCEPT MAX AND LEO *WITH THEIR BRILLIANCE,*
THEIR RESILIENCE,
UP TOGETHER THEY
WILL ZOOM!

MAX AND LEO *(shouting together, joyous and confident)*

We can't miss!

ALL EXCEPT MAX AND LEO *THEY WERE FATED,*
TO BE MATED,
THEY'RE BIALYSTOCK
AND BLOOM!
AHH! AHH!

MAX AND LEO *WE'RE BIALYSTOCK*
AND BLOOM!

The CURTAIN *falls as the signature chords of "Springtime for Hitler" are heard.*

END OF ACT ONE

ACT TWO ▪ SCENE 1

The ENTR'ACTE *ends as* MUSIC *segues into "When You Got It, Flaunt It," and the* CURTAIN *rises on the office, remarkably transformed into a miracle of Swedish "moderne," with a brand-new white desk replacing the old desk, a brand-new white couch replacing the old leather couch, etc., etc. Everything is gleamingly new, and all surfaces have been freshly painted a high-gloss Arctic white—white, white, everything is white.*

The time is late morning, a couple of days after the end of Act One. ULLA *is discovered alone on stage, up on a ladder, painting, putting the finishing touches on the new office. She is wearing a Sherwin-Williams painter's hat and a short sexy dress. After a few beats,* MAX *and* LEO *come bursting into the office.* MUSIC *out.*

MAX *(as they enter)*

We've gotta make that down payment on the theater by noon or else we . . .

(stopping and looking around in confusion)

Oh, sorry, wrong office.

MAX *and* LEO *hurry out, slamming the door behind them*

ULLA Bialystock . . . Bloom? Max, Leo?

After several beats of silence, the office door slowly opens and MAX *and* LEO *stick their heads in.*

MAX AND LEO Ulla?

ULLA *(brightly, cheerful)*

Ja.

MAX *(as he and* LEO *come in, leaving the door open behind them)*

What happened to the office?

ULLA Like you tell Ulla. Tidy up!

MAX Tidy up? When did you do all this?

ULLA *(very sing-songy Swedish reading)*

Inter-miss-ion.

MAX It figured.

(glancing at his watch)

Uh-oh, almost noon. Gotta make that payment to the Shuberts. I'll get the cash from the safe. You stay here and make sure all those contracts are signed!

(crosses over to safe and opens it)

ULLA *(to* LEO*)*

Gut tag pa dig.

LEO Gut tag pa dig.

MAX Hello, boys. Nobody knows what I went through to get you.

ULLA Ulla knows. You had to shtup every little old lady in New York.

MAX *(as he takes out a stack of bills and stuffs them in his pocket)*

That's right, and I've still got the denture bites to prove it.

(he closes the safe and exits, closing the open door)

ULLA *(she comes down the ladder to stand beside* LEO*)*

So, Mr. Bloom, ve're all alone.

LEO *(clearing his throat, nervously echoing her Swedish accent)*

Uh, yes, ve are, aren't ve? I mean, we are, aren't we?

ULLA Vhy Bloom go so far downstage right? Bloom no like Ulla? Ulla like Bloom.

LEO *(taking out his blue blanket)*

Oh, Bloom like Ulla all right. Maybe a little too much.

ULLA Gut, I'm glad. Why Bloom need blue blanket?

LEO It's not important. It's a minor compulsion. I've had it ever since I was a baby and . . . You're a little too close.

(MUSIC begins under as he gazes lovingly up at ULLA while she goes back to painting; sings)

THE URGE TO MERGE CAN ROB US OF OUR SENSES.
THE NEED TO BREED CAN MAKE A MAN A DRONE.
WE MUST BE ON ALERT WITH OUR DEFENSES.
FOR EVERY SKIRT WILL TEST TESTOSTERONE.

SO KNOWING THIS I SEVERED ALL CONNECTION
WITH ANY CREATURE SPORTING SILK OR LACE.
I WAS FIRMLY HEADED IN THE RIGHT DIRECTION . . .
WHEN SUDDENLY I STUMBLED ON . . . THAT FACE . . .

THAT FACE, THAT FACE, THAT DANGEROUS FACE,
I MUSTN'T BE UNWISE.
THOSE LIPS, THAT NOSE, THOSE EYES
COULD LEAD TO MY DEMISE.

THAT FACE, THAT FACE, THAT MARVELOUS FACE,
I NEVER SHOULD BEGIN,
THOSE CHEEKS, THAT NECK, THAT CHIN
WILL SURELY DO ME IN.

I MUST BE SMART,
AND HIDE MY HEART,
IF SHE'S WITHIN A MILE.
IF I DON'T DUCK,
I'M OUT OF LUCK,
SHE'D KILL ME WITH HER SMILE.

THAT FACE, THAT FACE, THAT FABULOUS FACE,
IT'S CLEAR I MUST BEWARE.

I'M CERTAIN IF I FALL IN LOVE
I'M LOST WITHOUT A TRACE
BUT IT'S WORTH IT . . . FOR THAT FACE.

ULLA *(calling to LEO as MUSIC continues)*

Uh-oh! Bloom help Ulla down?

LEO All right, Bloom help Ulla down.

ULLA comes down the ladder and into LEO'S arms. They dance à la Astaire-Rogers to an orchestral chorus of the song, after which they kiss.

Mel thought it would be a great idea to plaster Ulla's face on the white wall. It worked. Matthew's mother suggested that her baby boy's darling face be up there, too. It also worked.

ULLA *THAT FACE, THAT FACE, THAT LOVABLE FACE,*
IT MELTS MY SWEDISH HEART.

LEO *I'M CERTAIN IF I FALL IN LOVE*
I'M LOST WITHOUT A TRACE . . .

LEO AND ULLA *BUT IT'S WORTH IT FOR . . . THAT FACE.*

LEO *drops his blue blanket into the trash.* MAX *enters.*

MAX We're all set with the Shuberts! Bloom, what are you doing? Get back to cooking those books, one for the IRS, one for us.

MAX Bloom, what's the matter with you? Are you all right? You look happy.

LEO *crosses to the safe and takes out two large accounting ledgers.*

MAX *(picking up phone, then hanging up)*

I'll call you back.

(turning to spy ULLA, *who is leaning over to do a little touch-up painting; gazing at her gorgeous backside, he sings)*

THAT FACE, THAT FACE, THAT GLORIOUS FACE,
THIS GIRL IS TRULY BLESSED,
OHH-WAWAWOW IF SHE UNDRESSED,
IT'S CARDIAC ARREST.

ULLA *(standing up straight and glancing at her watch)*

Uh-oh, Bialystock and Bloom, you're late.

MAX Late? Late for what?

ULLA Auditions. You haf to go to auditions.

MAX AND LEO *(remembering)*

Ahhh. Auditions!

LEO *THAT FACE . . .*

MAX *THOSE FACE . . .*

MAX AND LEO *THAT WONDERFUL FACE,*
COULD REALLY DO SOME HARM.
BUT IT'S WORTH IT FOR THAT . . .

ULLA *(at the door, ready to leave, as* MUSIC *suspends)*

C'mon. Naughty boys, you ver late this morning. I vas vaiting for you ever since eleven.

MAX AND LEO Eleven!

(sing as MUSIC *resumes)*

FACE!

End of Act Two, Scene 1, as MAX, LEO, *and* ULLA *exit dancing à la Astaire-Rogers while* MUSIC *plays them off.* LIGHTS *and* SCENERY *change, and we segue into Scene 2.*

ACT TWO - SCENE 2

The bare stage of a Broadway theater. A producers' table on one side of the stage, an upright piano on the other.

Later the same day.

We hear the MUSIC *of "Keep It Gay" as the scrim rises to reveal the bare stage on which there are maybe a dozen dancing Hitlers. They are men—as well as women doubling as men—of all shapes and sizes, and in all sorts of ludicrous get-ups, each wearing a Hitler moustache. As the scene is revealed,* CARMEN *is leading the dancing Hitlers in a balletic dance audition. Meanwhile, a number of singing Hitlers, also wearing Hitler moustaches, are upstage shouting "Sieg Heil" over and over again while making the Nazi salute. A few are also loudly vocalizing.*

CARMEN Again! Arabesque, prepare, pirouette and twirl. And goosestep, goosestep, waltz, clog, and kick. Again! Arabesque, prepare, pirouette and twirl. And goosestep, goosestep, waltz, clog, and kick. Again! Arabesque, prepare, pirouette and twirl . . .

While the dancing Hitlers dance, ROGER *enters along with* FRANZ, *once again in his Nazi helmet and German black-leather military trench coat.* FRANZ *seats himself at the producers' table. An audition* PIANIST *is at the piano.* LEO, MAX, *and* ULLA, *who settle at the producers' table, are the last to enter.*

OPEN AUDITION TODAY FOR THE ROLE OF ADOLF HITLER NO PREVIOUS EXPERIENCE REQUIRED

ROGER *(having a hissy fit; stopping the audition)*

Haaalt!

CARMEN Halt!

ROGER Halt!

CARMEN Halt!

ROGER Oh, this is bedlam!

CARMEN Bedlam!

ROGER Bedlam!

CARMEN Bedlam! Settle people, settle!

ROGER We must have some order! Will the dancing Hitlers please go wait off-stage right. And the singing Hitlers off-stage left!

The DANCING HITLERS *go off-stage right and the* SINGING HITLERS *exit stage left.* MUSIC *out.*

Carmen, send in a singing Hitler, please.

CARMEN Yesss, Roger.

(announcing the first Hitler)

Jacques La-Pee-Dew, Jacques La-Pee-Dew?

*(*ROGER *looks at the card* CARMEN *is holding, then whispers into his ear)*

Jack Lapidus?

In Brooklyn, where Mel grew up, everyone named Lapidus had his name pronounced "La-pee-dus." But he was amazed when he went to Paris to discover that the famous French designer Ted Lapidus was known as Ted "La-pee-dew." The effete Carmen Ghia of course prefers "La-pee-dew," but no one, including Jack Lapidus himself, knows who the hell he is talking about.

JACK *walks to stand at stage center.*

ROGER Hello, Jack.

ROGER What are you going to sing for us?

JACK I would like to sing "A Wandering Minstrel, I."

ROGER (*unenthusiastic*)

If you must.

JACK (*nods to the* PIANIST, *who plays a brief intro, and then sings in a high tenor voice*)

AAAAAA, WANDERING MINSTREL, I,
A THING OF SHREDS AND . . .

ROGER (*dismissing* JACK)

Thank you!

JACK (*sings, unable to immediately stop*)

. . . PATCHES!

ROGER Next, please.

CARMEN (*calling out as* JACK *dejectedly exits*)

Donald Dinsmore.

ROGER (*as* DONALD *enters and goes to the stage-center mark*)

And what are you going to sing, Donald?

DONALD I would like to sing . . . "The Little Wooden Boy."

(*he nods to the* PIANIST, *who plays an elaborate intro to the song, in which he bounces like a doll, and then opens his mouth to sing*)

ROGER (*before* DONALD *has sung so much as a single note*)

Next!

(DONALD *discouragedly exits*)

CARMEN Jason Green!

JASON GREEN *enters and walks to the stage-center mark. He is a short, rotund man in a World War I German uniform and with a large handle-bar moustache.*

ROGER Well, Jason, what have you been up to lately?

JASON *(very actor-y, in a fake German accent)*

For the last sixteen years, I have been touring in "No, No, Nietzche."

ROGER You played Nietzche?

JASON No, no.

ROGER Hmm. And what are you going to sing?

JASON "Have You Ever Heard the German Band?"

ROGER No.

JASON That's the name of the song I'm going to sing.

ROGER Ohhh.

JASON *(turning toward the* PIANIST*)*

Play it, please.

The PIANIST *plays a brief intro and* JASON *sings in very bad American-sounding German.*

HABEN SIE GEHOERT DAS DEUTSCHE BAND,
MIT A BANG, MIT A BOOM,
MIT A BING-BANG BING-BANG BOOM!
OH, HABEN SIE GEHORT . . . .

FRANZ *(standing and angrily shouting in the middle of* JASON*'s audition)*

Halt! Halt! This man could never play Adolf Hitler! Der Führer vasn't a mousy little mama's boy. Der Führer vas butch! And that is not how you sing "Haben Sie Gehoert Das Deutsche Band." This

is how you sing "Haben Sie Gehoert Das Deutsche Band." B-flat. Two-two time. Modulate at the bridge!

FRANZ *scares* JASON *and* JASON *runs off.*

(he sings, at the top of his lungs; in very German German and in a Jolson-like vaudeville style)

HABEN SIE GEHOERT DAS DEUTSCHE BAND,
MIT A BANG, MIT A BOOM,
MIT A BING-BANG BING-BANG BOOM!

OOOH, HABEN SIE GEHOERT DAS DEUTSCHE BAND,
MIT A BANG, MIT A BOOM,
MIT A BING-BANG BING-BANG BOOM!
RUSSIAN FOLK SONGS AND FRENCH OO-LA-LA
CAN'T COMPARE TO THAT GERMAN OOM-PAH-PAH!

VE'RE SAYIN' . . .

HABEN SIE GEHOERT DAS DEUTSCHE BAND . . .
MIT A ZETZ, MIT A ZAP, MIT A ZING . . .

POLISH POLKAS, THEY'RE STUPID AND THEY'RE ROTTEN,
IT DON'T MEAN A THING IF IT AIN'T GOT THAT
SCHWEIGEN-REIGEN-SCHONE-SCHUTZEN-SCHMUTZEN
SAUERBRATEN!

Key change!

VE'RE SAYIN' . . .

HABEN SIE GEHOERT DAS DEUTSCHE BAND . . .

MIT A ZETZ, MIT A ZAP, MIT A ZING . . .
IT'S THE ONLY KIND OF MUSIK
THAT VE HUNS AND OUR HONEYS LOVE TO SING!

MAX *(leaping to his feet and pointing at* FRANZ*)*

That's our Hitler!!

MUSIC *up, the closing notes of "Haben Sie Gehoert Das Deutsche Band" as Scene 2 ends,* LIGHTS *and* SCENERY *begin to change, and we segue into . . .*

ACT TWO ▪ SCENE 3

The exterior of the Shubert Theatre, as viewed from West 44th Street, with Shubert Alley at stage left. Early on a Thursday evening, several weeks later, mid-September.

The marquee of the theater has a sign saying, "Bialystock and Bloom Present 'Springtime for Hitler, A Gay Romp with Adolf and Eva in Berchtesgaden.'"

The MUSIC *of "You Never Say 'Good Luck' on Opening Night" plays under the scene change and then out as the two uniformed* USHERETTES *who opened the show in Act One enter.*

USHERETTES #1 AND #2 *OPENING NIGHT . . .*
. . . IT'S OPENING NIGHT!
IT'S MAX BIALYSTOCK'S LATEST SHOW.
WILL IT FLOP OR WILL IT GO?

THE HOUSE LIGHTS ARE DIMMING,
THE FOOTLIGHTS ARE BRIGHT,
THE TOAST OF SOCIETY'S BURNING TONIGHT!

WE'RE SO EXCITED WE CAN'T SIT DOWN
'CAUSE "SPRINGTIME FOR HITLER" HAS COME TO TOWN!

Now, the same WORKMAN *who appeared in Act One, Scene 1, enters from Shubert Alley with the sign saying "Opening Night." He checks to see—as the audience also sees—that it says "Closing Night" on its reverse side. He then hangs it up, gives the audience a knowing look, and exits back into Shubert Alley, where there is a sign with an arrow saying "To Stage Door."*

The lights on the theater now come on brighter, the MUSIC *of "You Never Say 'Good Luck' on Opening Night" again begins under, and a horde of* FIRST NIGHTERS *in evening clothes enters from all sides, as a* TICKET TAKER *in a hat and a tuxedo appears by the door leading to the theater's lobby and begins taking tickets.*

TICKET TAKER Have your tickets ready. Have your tickets ready! This way please, this way. Please take your seats.

During the above, MAX, *in his tuxedo and battered producer's hat, enters from Shubert Alley, while* LEO, *also in a tuxedo and starting to put on a producer's hat, enters opposite.* MUSIC *out.*

MAX Whoa, Bloom, who said you could wear that hat?

LEO Nobody, Max. But now that I'm the producer of . . .

SHUBERT THEATRE
BIALYSTOCK
& BLOOM
PRESENT
SPRINGTIME
FOR HITLER
OPENING NIGHT

MAX Has the curtain gone up yet?

LEO No.

MAX Has the curtain come down yet?

LEO No.

MAX Then you're not a producer yet.

(grabbing the hat from LEO*)*

Gimme that hat!

ULLA, *dressed as "a late showgirl," hurries on from stage right and goes up to* LEO, *whose tie is lopsided.*

ULLA Oh, Mr. Bloom, Leo, your tie is all askew.

LEO Askew?

(as ULLA *straightens his tie and gives him a kiss)*

Thank you, Ulla. Have a good show. Roll 'em in the aisles.

ULLA Okey dokey, I will try to, but there's just so many of them.

MAX *(aside to* LEO *as* ULLA *exits stage left into Shubert Alley)*

I thought we were partners, sharing everything fifty-fifty. Now I'm out in the cold and you two are busy askewing each other.

LEO Askewing! Never, Max. Hugs and kisses, yes, but that's as far as I go.

MAX I believe it.

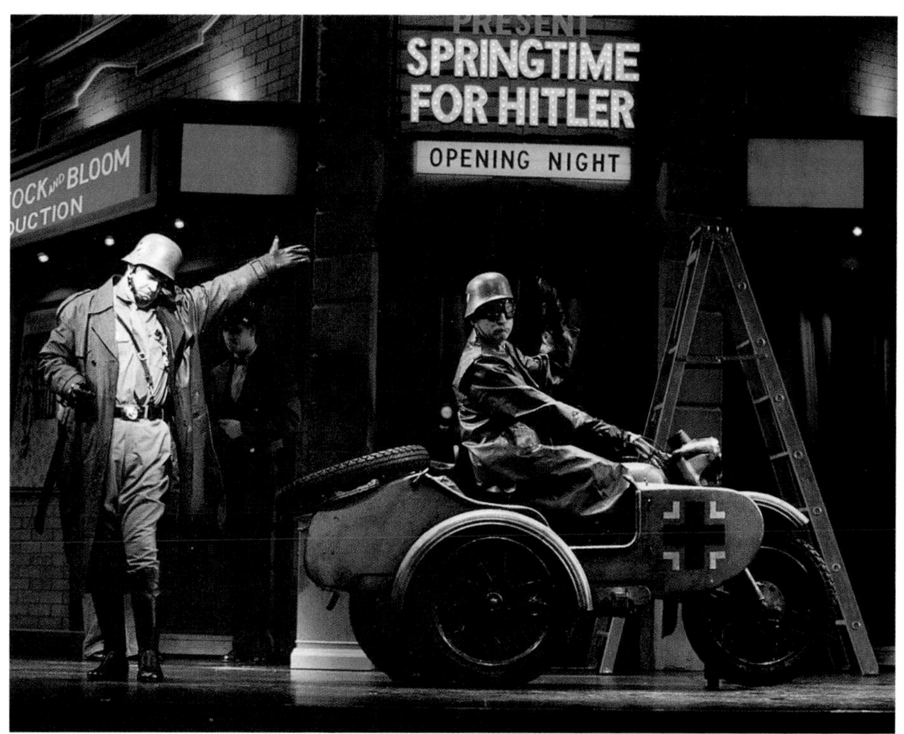

MUSIC*: "The Guten Tag Hop Clop" as* FRANZ*, in his German helmet and leather coat, comes roaring on stage seated in the sidecar of a motorcycle driven by a driver (*GUNTER*) in a black jump suit and dark sunglasses and also wearing a German helmet. The motorcycle screeches to a halt in front of the theater and* FRANZ *leaps out.* MUSIC*: Out.*

FRANZ Gunter, you vill pick me up back here right after the curtain, jawohl?

GUNTER Jawohl, mein Herr!

GUNTER *roars off on the motorcycle as* FRANZ *goes to* MAX *and* LEO.

MAX Franz, what are you doing? It's almost half-hour. You should be ready to go on.

FRANZ I am ready. All I have to do is change my hat and slap on my Hitler moustache.

By now, all of the FIRST NIGHTERS *have hastened into the theater as* ROGER *and* CARMEN *enter in evening clothes, all atwitter.*

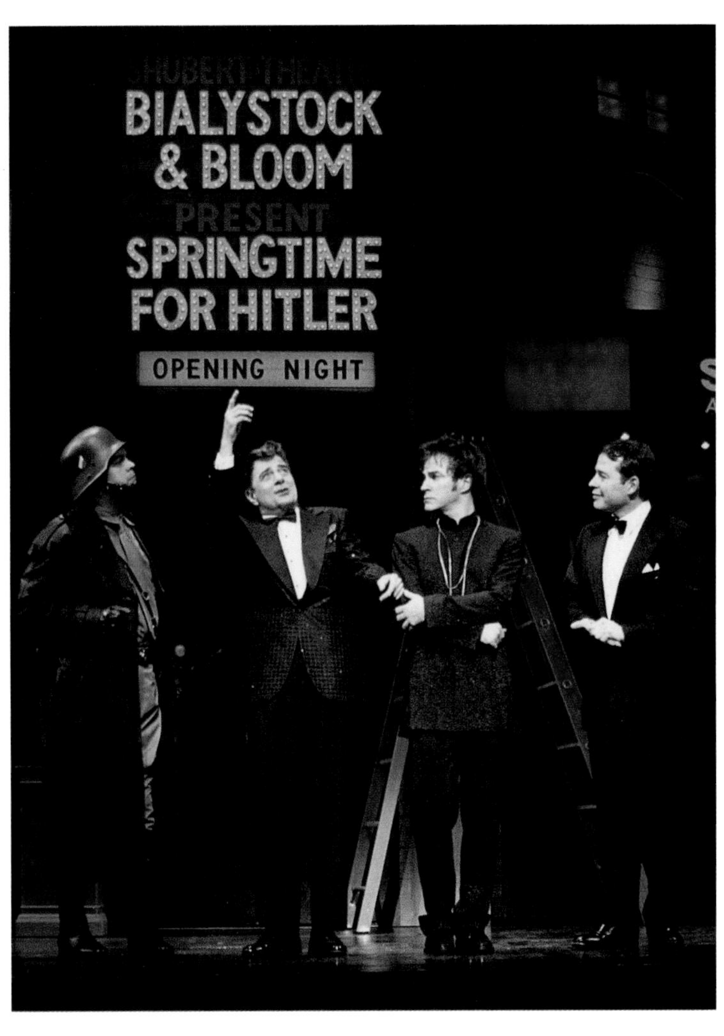

ROGER Oh, God, will they love us, will they hate us, the suspense is killing me.

CARMEN I know. I feel like I'm going into labor. Hoo, hoo, hoo, hoo.

ROGER Ah, it's Bialystock and Bloom. Well, gentlemen . . . merde!

CARMEN Tu, tu, tu.

FRANZ Hals und Beine brüch!

LEO And I just want to wish everybody . . . good luck!

MUSIC: *A sting of alarm and then an intro to "You Never Say 'Good Luck' on Opening Night" begins under.*

ROGER *(aghast)*

What?! What did you say?

CARMEN *(equally aghast)*

Bite your tongue!

FRANZ Gott in Himmel!

LEO What's the matter? All I said was, "Good luck."

CARMEN *(in a high-pitched shriek)*

Ahhhh! He said it again!!

ROGER *(as the* **MUSIC** *of "You Never Say 'Good Luck' on Opening Night" begins)*

Mr. Bloom, hasn't anyone ever told you . . .

IT'S BAD LUCK TO SAY "GOOD LUCK" ON OPENING NIGHT.
IF YOU DO, I TELL YOU,
IT IS CERTAIN BY THE CURTAIN
YOU ARE THROUGH!

MAX *(at stage right, greeting cast and crew members heading down Shubert Alley toward the stage door)*

Good luck!

CARMEN *IT'S BAD LUCK TO SAY "GOOD LUCK" ON OPENING NIGHT.*
ONCE IT'S SAID, YOU ARE DEAD,
YOU WILL GET THE WORST REVIEWS
YOU'VE EVER READ!

MAX Good luck!

ROGER *EVEN AT THE COMÉDIE FRANÇAISE,*
ON THE OPENING NIGHT THEY ARE SCARED.

Several late **CHORUS GIRLS** *enter.*

"BONNE CHANCE," MES AMIS, NO ONE SAYS,
THE ONLY WORD YOU'LL EVER HEAR IS . . .

ROGER, CARMEN, AND FRANZ *MERDE!*

MAX Good luck, good luck, good luck.

LATE CHORUS GIRLS *(shriek)*

Aah!

(they exit)

FRANZ *IT'S VERBOTEN VISHING "LUCK" ON OPENING NIGHT,*
TAKE ADVICE, DON'T THINK TWICE,
OR YOUR SHOW WILL SURELY END
UP IN THE SCHEISS!

MAX *(mock German)*

Guten lucken.

CARMEN *AT THE FAMOUS LA SCALA IN MILAN*
ON OPENING NIGHT IT'S A RULE.

"IN BOCA LUPA" THEY SAY WITH ÉLAN,
AND JUST FOR LUCK THEY ALL SHOUT . . .

ROGER, CARMEN, AND FRANZ *"BAH FONGOOL!"*

LEO I got it!

NOW I'LL NEVER SAY "GOOD LUCK" ON OPENING NIGHT,
THAT'S THE RULE, I'M NO FOOL!
WHAT DO I SAY, I BEG?

ROGER, CARMEN, AND FRANZ *WHAT YOU SAY IS "BREAK A LEG!"*

LEO Break a leg?

ROGER, CARMEN, AND FRANZ Yes, break a leg!

LEO, ROGER, CARMEN, AND FRANZ *IF YOU'RE CLEVER . . .*

MAX Good luck!

LEO, ROGER, CARMEN, AND FRANZ *YOU'LL ENDEAVOR . . .*

MAX *kicks and shatters the mirror carried by a stagehand.*

LEO, ROGER, CARMEN, AND FRANZ *TO NEVER, NEVER, NEVER, NEVER, EVER, EVER, EVER,*
SAY . . .

Very trivial trivia. Don't tell anybody, but the prerecorded sound of the screeching cat was performed by Mel Brooks.

MAX *picks up a black cat and throws it; the cat screeches in the rhythm of "good luck."*

. . . ON OPENING NIGHT!!

TICKET TAKER *(following the end of the number)*

Five minutes to curtain. Curtain going up in five minutes.

FRANZ Hassenpfeffer! I'm late! I muzt run!

ALL *(as* FRANZ *runs off)*

Break a leg!

FRANZ *runs off down Shubert Alley and goes in the stage door, out of sight of the audience. There is the sound of a long crash and* FRANZ *yelling.*

MAX *(calling toward the stage door)*

Franz! Franz, what happened?

FRANZ *(calling from stage door)*

I broke my leg!

ROGER Oh, my God, no! We'll have to cancel the show and give everyone their money back.

MAX Money back? Never! We've gotta think of something else.

LEO But Franz plays Hitler and he has no understudy.

MAX You're right. What're we gonna do? I've got to think of something . . . Hold it! I've got it! Roger, you could play Hitler! You know every line in the show. I've seen you at rehearsal, always moving your lips along with the actors.

ROGER I know. It's such an embarrassing habit. I'm trying to break myself of it. But me play Hitler? No, there's no way I could go on tonight. I don't have the strength. I don't have the courage. I can't do it, I can't do it, I can't do it!

(CARMEN *slaps him across the face)*

Ow! That hurt.

CARMEN Roger, listen to me

*(*MUSIC *of "Keep It Gay" quietly under the following speech)*

Our affectionate little salute to 42nd Street.

You can do it, you know you can do it, and I know you can do it. You've been waiting all your life for this chance. And I'm not going to let you pass it up. You're going out there a silly hysterical screaming queen and you're coming back a great big passing-for-straight Broadway star!!

ROGER All right, you're right! I'll do it! By God, I'll do it! I've got to get into makeup!

(he runs off down Shubert Alley, calling back to CARMEN*)*

Quick, get me Franz's Hitler moustache and, oh, my lucky Gloria Swanson mole!

CARMEN Got it!

(he and ROGER *exit)*

MAX *(as the* MUSIC *of the overture to* Springtime for Hitler *begins inside the theater)*

The overture! Let's go.

LEO Max!

MAX What?

LEO This is it!

MAX Good luck, Leo!

LEO Good luck, Max!

MUSIC: *The Overture to* Springtime for Hitler *comes up loud as* MAX *and* LEO *exit into the theater. The scene ends as a* Springtime for Hitler *show curtain comes in.*

ACT TWO - SCENE 4

We see the garish and kitschy Springtime for Hitler *show curtain as the* MUSIC *of the show's overture continues to a big finish. A minute or so after the end of Scene 3. As the overture ends, the show curtain rises on a* CHORUS *of six men and six women in traditional Bavarian peasant costumes standing in front of an Alpine drop.*

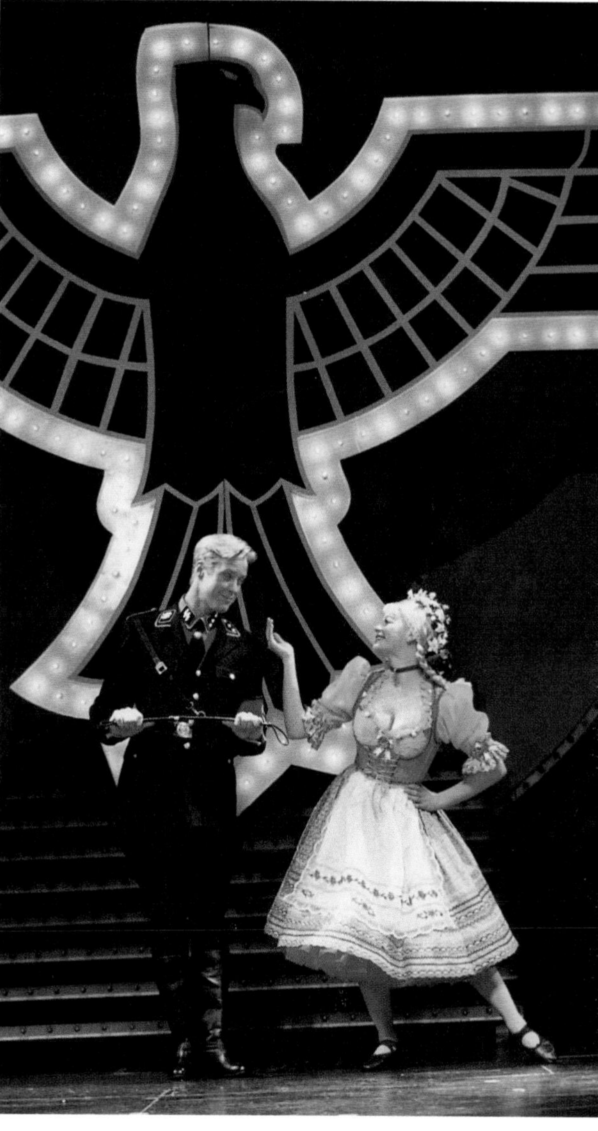

CHORUS *GERMANY WAS HAVING TROUBLE,*
WHAT A SAD, SAD STORY.
NEEDED A NEW LEADER TO RESTORE
IT'S FORMER GLORY.
WHERE, OH, WHERE WAS HE?
WHERE COULD THAT MAN BE?
WE LOOKED AROUND AND THEN WE FOUND,
THE MAN FOR YOU AND ME,

WHERE, OH, WHERE WAS HE?
WHERE COULD THAT MAN BE?
WE LOOKED AROUND AND THEN WE FOUND,
THE MAN FOR YOU AND ME.

The drop now rises as the CHORUS *exits to reveal a large staircase, upstage center, at the bottom of which stands a* STORM TROOPER *in full Nazi uniform. The stairs are elaborately flanked on each side by five scantily clad Ziegfeld Follies-like girls in frozen poses. One of them, we see, is* ULLA.

STORM TROOPER *AND NOW IT'S . . .*
SPRINGTIME FOR HITLER AND GERMANY . . .

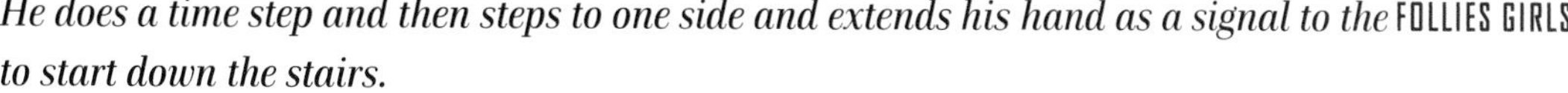

He does a time step and then steps to one side and extends his hand as a signal to the FOLLIES GIRLS *to start down the stairs.*

STORM TROOPER *DEUTCHLAND IS HAPPY AND . . .*

*(*FOLLIES GIRL #1, *with a beer mug on her head and one on each bosom, descends the stairs)*

. . . GAY!

WE'RE MARCHING TO A . . .

*(*FOLLIES GIRL #2, *in an elaborate Valkyrie outfit, wearing long gold braids, descends the stairs)*

. . . FASTER PACE . . .

(as the STORM TROOPER *takes* FOLLIES GIRL #2 *and guides her down the stairs)*

. . . LOOK OUT, HERE COMES THE . . .

*(*FOLLIES GIRL #3*, with a large pretzel on her head and pretzels on her bosoms, descends)*

. . . MASTER RACE!

*(*FOLLIES GIRL #4*, with bratwurst on her head and sausages on each bosom, descends the stairs)*

SPRINGTIME . . .
. . . FOR HITLER AND GERMANY,
RHINELAND'S A FINE LAND ONCE MORE!

SPRINGTIME FOR HITLER AND . . .
GERMANY . . .
WATCH OUT, EUROPE,
WE'RE GOING ON TOUR!

SPRINGTIME . . .
. . . FOR HITLER AND GERMANY,

CHORUS *LOOK, IT'S SPRINGTIME!*

STORM TROOPER *WINTER FOR POLAND*
AND FRANCE.

CHORUS *OOOHH!*
AAAHH!

CHORUS AND STORM TROOPER *SPRINGTIME FOR HITLER AND . . .*

(as he leads ULLA*, who is* FOLLIES GIRL #5*, wearing a winged German eagle on her head and swastikas on her bosoms, descends the stairs)*

. . . GERMANY!

CHORUS *SPRINGTIME! SPRINGTIME!*
SPRINGTIME! SPRINGTIME!
SPRINGTIME! SPRINGTIME!
SPRINGTIME! SPRINGTIME!

STORM TROOPER *COME ON, GERMANS, GO . . .*
. . . INTO YOUR DANCE!

A squad of STORM TROOPERS, *men and women, enter and dance.*

STORM TROOPER "ROLF" *(speaking out front in a dance break)*

I was born in Düsseldorf and that is why they call me Rolf.

In Chicago, at least half of the audience each night seemed to think that Mel was actually on stage doing this bit and gave the line a huge hand. The real actor doing it, Peter Marinos, hearing so much applause on his exit, asked for a raise.

STORM TROOPER "MEL" *(speaking out front in a second dance break, lip-synching to a voice-over of* MEL BROOKS*)*

Don't be stupid, be a smarty, come and join the Nazi party!

The STORM TROOPERS' *dance continues to a finish.*

ULLA *(chanting as* MUSIC *continues)*

The Führer is coming, the Führer is coming, the Führer is coming!

(she exits)

STORM TROOPER "ROLF" Heil Hitler!

STORM TROOPER "MEL" Heil Hitler!

STORM TROOPERS "MEL" AND "ROLF" Heil Hitler!

STORM TROOPERS *SPRINGTIME FOR HITLER AND GERMANY . . . !*

ROGER DE BRIS, *as* HITLER, *enters at the top of the stairs.*

ALL Heil Hitler!

ROGER *HEIL MYSELF,*
HEIL TO ME,
I'M THE KRAUT WHO'S OUT TO CHANGE OUR HISTORY!

HEIL MYSELF,
RAISE YOUR HAND,
THERE'S NO GREATER . . . DICTATOR IN THE LAND!

EVERYTHING I DO, I DO FOR YOU!

CHORUS *YES, YOU DO!*

ROGER *IF YOU'RE LOOKING FOR A WAR, HERE'S WORLD WAR TWO!*
HEIL MYSELF,
RAISE YOUR BEER!

CHORUS *JAWOHL!!*

ROGER *EV'RY HOTSY-TOTSY NAZI STAND AND CHEER!*

CHORUS *HURRAY!*
EV'RY HOTSY-TOTSY NAZI . . .

ROGER *HEIL MYSELF!*

CHORUS *EV'RY HOTSY-TOTSY NAZI . . .*

ROGER *HEIL MYSELF!*

CHORUS *EV'RY HOTSY-TOTSY NAZI . . .*

ROGER *. . . STAND AND CHEER!*

THE HEIL-LOS, *a chorus of two women and three men, sing and dance with* ROGER *during the following section as all others exit.*

THE HEIL-LOS *THE FÜHRER IS CAUSING A FUROR!*

HEIL-LO WOMEN		HEIL-LO MEN	
	HE'S GOT THOSE RUSSIANS ON THE RUN,		*OOH!*
	YOU GOTTA LOVE THAT WACKY HUN!		*OOH!*

THE HEIL-LOS *THE FÜHRER IS CAUSING A FUROR!*
THEY CAN'T SAY "NO" TO HIS DEMANDS,
THEY'RE FREAKING OUT IN FOREIGN LANDS,
HE'S GOT THE WHOLE WORLD IN HIS HANDS.

THE FÜHRER IS CAUSING A FUROR!
OOH-OOH
OOH-OOH
OOH-OOH
OOH-OOH
AAH!

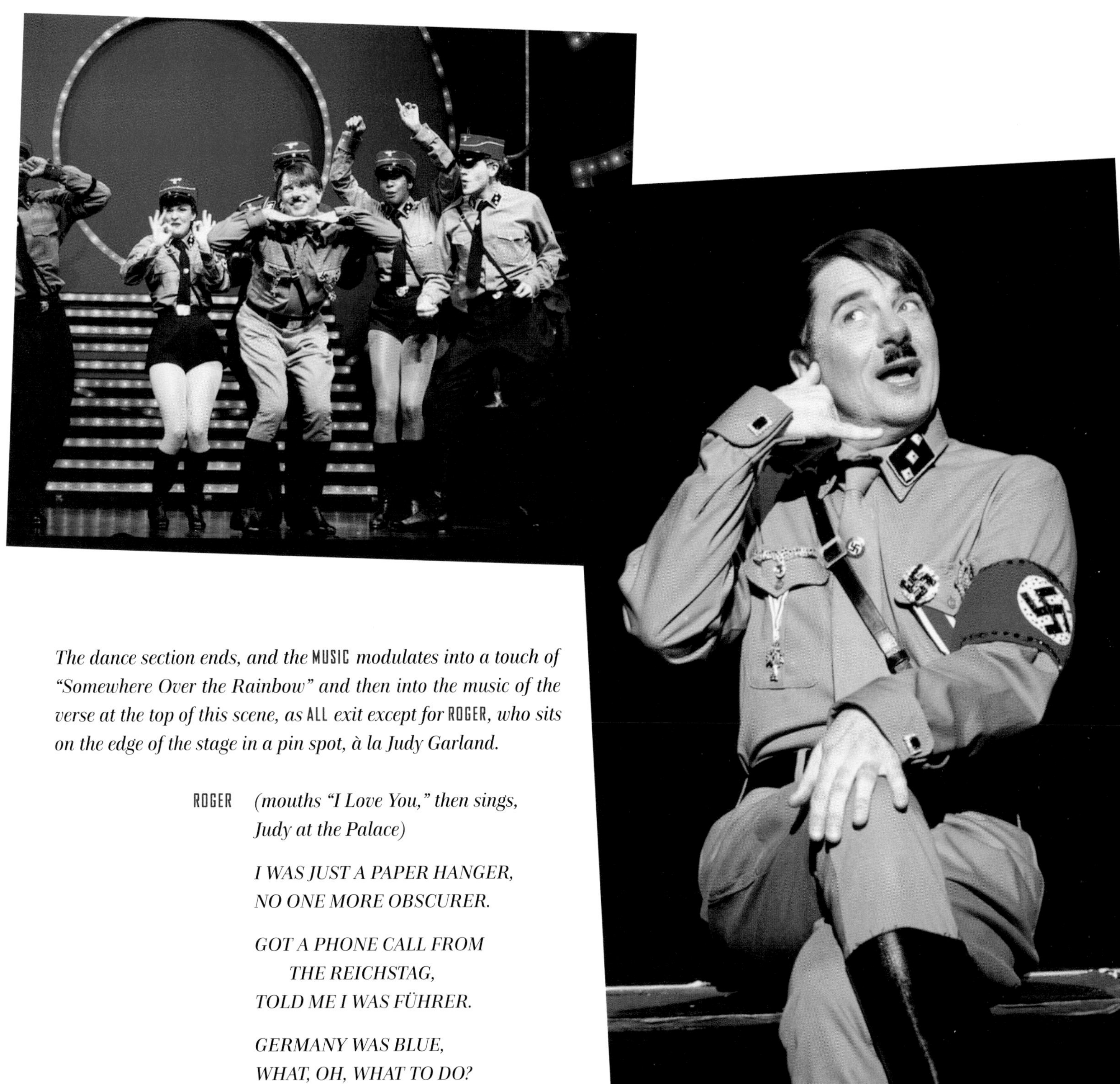

The dance section ends, and the MUSIC *modulates into a touch of "Somewhere Over the Rainbow" and then into the music of the verse at the top of this scene, as* ALL *exit except for* ROGER, *who sits on the edge of the stage in a pin spot, à la Judy Garland.*

ROGER *(mouths "I Love You," then sings, Judy at the Palace)*

I WAS JUST A PAPER HANGER,
NO ONE MORE OBSCURER.

GOT A PHONE CALL FROM
THE REICHSTAG,
TOLD ME I WAS FÜHRER.

GERMANY WAS BLUE,
WHAT, OH, WHAT TO DO?

HITCHED UP MY PANTS
AND CONQUERED FRANCE . . .

NOW DEUTSCHLAND'S SMILING
THROUGH!

ULLA *(as she enters)*

CHALLENGE TAP, CHALLENGE TAP,
ADOLF DIGS A CHALLENGE TAP!

ULLA *dances.*

ULLA *BRING ON THE ALLIES TO HEAR THE NEWS . . .*
THE FACTS IS THE AXIS CANNOT LOSE!

'CAUSE MR. H . . .

ROGER Who is that?

ULLA *MR. H . . .*

ROGER That's me!

ULLA *IS WEARING HIS DANCING SHOES!*

(she exits)

ROGER *now does a few tap steps. An ensemble member made up as* STALIN *enters to the* MUSIC *of "The Volga Boat Song."*

STALIN *I AM STALIN. YOU'LL SOON BE FALLIN'. HA!*

STALIN *tap dances heavy-footedly, making a poor attempt at a buck-and-wing to the* MUSIC. ROGER *then does a terrific buck-and-wing.* STALIN, *defeated, exits.*

An ensemble member made up as CHURCHILL *enters to the* MUSIC *of "Rule, Britannia!"*

CHURCHILL *I AM CHURCHILL. I AM HERE TO WIN THE DAY!*

He tries to tap to the MUSIC *but is no match for* ROGER, *who literally tap dances circles around him. Defeated,* CHURCHILL *exits.*

Finally, an ensemble member made up as FDR *enters in a wheelchair to the* MUSIC *of "America the Beautiful." He taps mini American flags on his wheel.*

ROGER *shoves the wheelchair and sends it speeding off into the wings.*

ROGER *IT AIN'T NO MYST'RY,*
IF IT'S POLITICS OR HIST'RY.
THE THING YOU GOTTA KNOW IS,
EV'RYTHING IS SHOW BIZ.

HEIL MYSELF
WATCH MY SHOW
I'M THE GERMAN ETHEL
MERMAN, DONTCHA KNOW!

WE ARE CROSSING BORDERS
THE NEW WORLD ORDER IS HERE
MAKE A GREAT BIG SMILE
EV'RY-ONE SIEG HIEL TO ME
WONDERFUL ME!

AND NOW IT'S . . .

ROGER *laughs as he is joined now by the dancing* STORM TROOPERS *along with a group of dancing, scantily clad* BLACK-SHIRTED GIRLS. ALL *swing into a further instrumental dance chorus. There is a lot of linking of arms, high-kicking, Nazi saluting, and danced goose-stepping. This leads into the return of the* CHORUS *and final chorus of the song.*

CHORUS *SPRINGTIME FOR HITLER AND GERMANY . . .*

ROGER *SPRINGTIME!*

The DANCERS *freeze in step as there is the* SOUND OF MACHINE-GUN SHOTS *and then continue dancing when the burst of* SHOTS *ends.*

CHORUS *. . . GOOSE-STEP'S THE NEW STEP TODAY.*

ROGER *GOOSE-STEPS!*

CHORUS MEN *BOMBS FALLING FROM THE SKIES AGAIN . . .*

CHORUS *. . . DEUTSCHLAND IS ON THE RISE AGAIN.*

The DANCERS *form a swastika that the audience sees reflected in a tilted upstage mirror. The swastika rotates clockwise.*

ROGER AND CHORUS *SPRINGTIME FOR HITLER AND GERMANY . . .*
U-BOATS ARE SAILING ONCE MORE.

SPRINGTIME FOR HITLER AND GERMANY!

ROGER *MEANS THAT . . . .*

CHORUS *SOON WE'LL BE GOING . . .*

ROGER *WE'VE GOT TO BE GOING . . .*

For a big finish, columns on stage swing down to face the audience and fire like cannons; meanwhile, PARATROOPERS *drop in from above at the very end of the number as a pair of* AFRIKA CORPS TANKS *(actors in papier-mâché constructions, à la* The Lion King*) enter. And, finally, a half-globe of the world comes up from the stage, and* ROGER *as Hitler stands on top of it. Meanwhile,* ULLA, *having exited and changed into a tight-fitting silver-lamé Nazi outfit, tap dances about à la Eleanor Powell.*

CHORUS *YOU KNOW WE'LL BE GOING . . .*

ROGER *YOU BET WE'LL BE GOING . . .*

ROGER AND CHORUS *YOU KNOW WE'LL BE GOING TO . . .*
WAR!!!
AAH!!!

The Springtime for Hitler *show curtain falls as the number ends. The* MUSIC *of "Springtime for Hitler" then again strikes up as* ALL, *led by* ROGER, *come out in front of the curtain to take bows for their triumphant performance.* CARMEN *comes down the aisle of the theater carrying a huge bouquet of roses that he presents to a tearfully joyous* ROGER. ROGER, *however, doesn't embrace* CARMEN *but instead embraces* ULLA, *and we see that he is "passing for straight."* MUSIC *plays* ROGER *and the cast off as they exit, waving and blowing kisses to the audience, as Scene 4 ends and we segue into . . .*

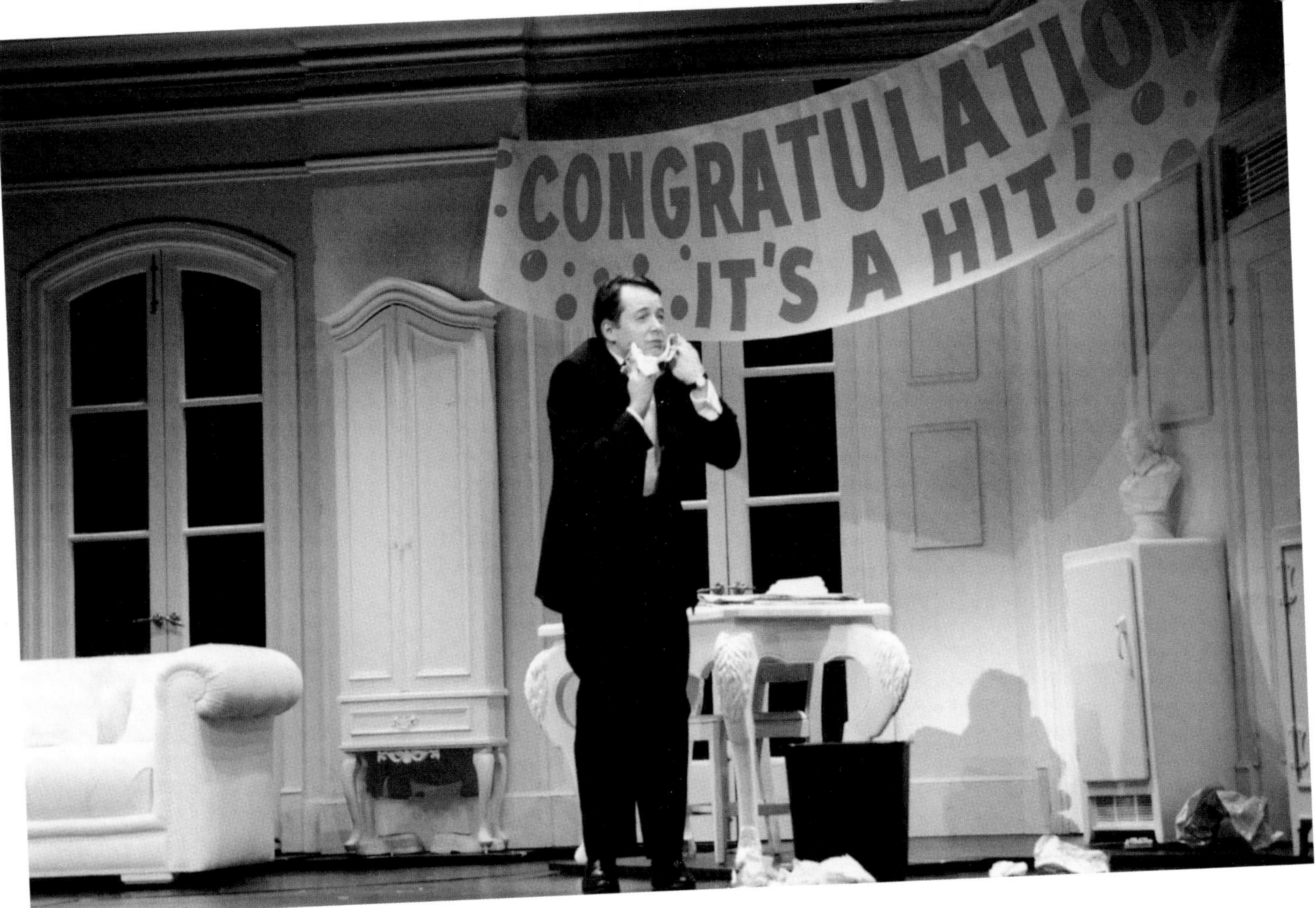

ACT TWO - SCENE 5

The Springtime for Hitler *show curtain rises to reveal the office. Later that night, around midnight.* MUSIC *segues into "Springtime for Hitler" arranged as a dirge and plays under the beginning of the scene.*

LEO *enters, stunned and shocked. A handmade sign saying "Congratulations!" is strung across the room. Meanwhile,* MAX *enters reading from newspapers.*

MAX *(reading from one of the papers as the* MUSIC *of "Where Did We Go Right?" begins under)*

"A satiric masterpiece."

LEO No way out.

MAX *(reading from another of the papers)*

"A surprise smash!"

LEO No way out.

MAX *(reading from yet another of the papers)*

"It was shocking, outrageous, insulting, . . . and I loved every minute of it!"

LEO No way out.

MAX *HOW COULD THIS HAPPEN?*

THE SHOW WAS LOUSY AND LONG,
WE DID EVERYTHING WRONG,
WHERE DID WE GO RIGHT?

LEO *(reading from yet another review)*

"Christmas came early to Broadway this season—and guess who they stuffed in our stocking? Adolf Hitler!"

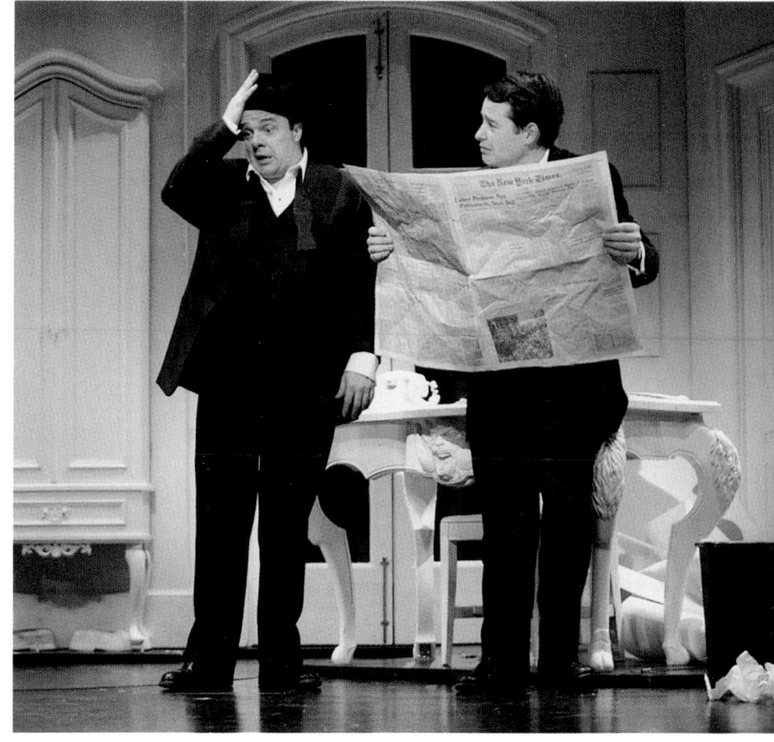

MAX *IT WAS SO CRASS AND SO CRUDE,*
EVEN GOEBBELS WOULD'VE
BOOED,
WHERE DID WE GO RIGHT?

LEO *(again reading from another review)*

"Last night a new star was born on Broadway—the lovely Miss Ulla Inga Hansen Bensen Yonsen Tallen-Hallen *(*LEO *turns the page)* Svaden-Svanson. We predict that her name will soon be up in lights. If they can find enough bulbs."

MAX AND LEO *WE SEARCHED BROADWAY ON AND OFF,*
FOR SINGERS WITH A COUGH,
WE HAD TRYOUTS AND AUDITIONS BY THE SCORE.

AND TO TRIP THE LIGHT FANTASTIC,
WE PICKED DANCERS WHO WERE SPASTIC,
IF ANYONE JETÉ'D
WE JETÉ'D THEM OUT THE DOOR!

MAX *THEY SHOUTED HURRAY,*
FOR THAT SAUSAGE ON DISPLAY,
WHERE DID WE GO RIGHT?

LEO *OUR LEADING MAN WAS SO GAY*
HE NEARLY FLEW AWAY
WHERE DID WE GO RIGHT?

MAX *A SHOW SO EASY TO DESPISE . . .*

LEO *NOW IT'S UP FOR THE PULITZER PRIZE!*

MAX AND LEO *OH, WHERE, OH, WHERE, TELL US WHERE*
DID WE GO RIGHT?

MAX *(reading yet another review)*

"The best new musical of the decade! Max Bialystock is a theatrical genius!" Now they like me.

MAX *OH, WE KNEW WE COULDN'T LOSE,*

MAX AND LEO *HALF THE AUDIENCE WERE JEWS!*

LEO *IT'S THE END OF OUR CAREERS,*

MAX *IT'LL RUN FOR TWENTY YEARS!*

MAX AND LEO *TELL US WHERE . . .*
DID WE GO RIGHT?!

On the applause for the number, LEO *goes to the safe, opens it, and takes out two large accounting ledgers. He closes the safe and heads for the door.*

MAX What are you doing? What are you doing?

LEO I'm taking these books and I'm leaving. Don't try to stop me. I've made up my mind.

MAX Where do think you're going?

LEO I'm turning myself in. It's the only way. I'm going to cooperate with the authorities. They'll reduce my sentence and then there's time off for good behavior. Maybe I'll get a good job in the prison library.

(again heading for the door)

Keep in touch. It's been very nice working with you.

MAX Leo, Leo, Leo, Leo. Frightened Leo, nervous Leo, take it easy. Relax, you're overwrought. You don't know what you're doing. You're acting out of panic.

(yells)

Gimme those books!

(he starts to wrestle the books away from LEO*)*

LEO I never should have listened to you. I was an honest man before I met you.

MAX An honest man! You were an honest mouse!

LEO Ooohhhhh, how I hate you!

MAX Double, double, double!

(MAX succeeds in ripping the books out of LEO's hands)

Haaaaa! Ha-ha haaaaa!

Nathan Lane had worked incredibly hard in rehearsal, in Chicago, and during the first several months on stage in New York. He'd dropped so many pounds we were thinking of changing this line to "Skin-skin-skinny!"

LEO slaps his hands on MAX's cheeks, pulls MAX's hat ludicrously down over his ears, and yells hysterically at him. MAX falls to the floor.

LEO Fat! Fat! Fat! Fat! Fatty!

(he jumps on MAX's back on the floor and grapples to get the books back)

Just gimme those fat books, you fat walrus!

MAX Never!

MAX and LEO are on the floor, fighting, as ROGER now bursts in with CARMEN. They are in joyous and triumphant spirits.

LEO	Give it to me!	**MAX**	No!		
	Give it to me!		No!	**ROGER**	Congratulations!
	Give it to me!		No!		
	Give it to me!		No!	**CARMEN**	Congratulations!
	Give it to me!		No!		
	Give it to me!		No!	**ROGER**	Congrat . . .
	Give it to me!		No!		

ROGER Now that's what I call celebrating!

MAX *(to ROGER; shouting from the floor)*

You lousy fruit, you ruined me!

CARMEN Why, you ungrateful breeder, after he stepped in and saved your show!

FRANZ now enters on one crutch, with his right leg in a cast, brandishing a Luger.

FRANZ Aah! You haf broken the Siegfried Oath! You all must die!

ALL now scramble for safety as FRANZ starts wildly shooting and bullets fly in all directions. ALL shriek with fear and race about like poulets with their têtes cut off. MUSIC under.

ROGER What are you doing, you neo-Nazi nitwit? Your show's a hit!

FRANZ Who cares? You made a fool out of Hitler!

ROGER AND CARMEN He didn't need our help!

MUSIC *up as* FRANZ *continues wildly shooting but missing.* ROGER, CARMEN, *and* MAX *exit out onto the balcony.* FRANZ *follows.* LEO *opens the stage-left patio door and* MAX, CARMEN, ROGER *and* FRANZ *enter.* ROGER *and* CARMEN *cross to the stage-right closet.* MAX *and* LEO *duck under the desk.*

ROGER *(opens closet door for* CARMEN*)*

Darling, back in the closet.

CARMEN Okay.

FRANZ All right, Bialystock und Bloom, now I got you. Say your prayers.

MAX *(to* LEO*)*

Remember I told you I'd tell you when we're in too deep?

LEO Yes.

MAX We're in too deep.

FRANZ Auf Wiedersehen! . . .

MAX and LEO begin to cry

FRANZ . . . Ach, you sniveling cowards, I show you how to die like a man.

(FRANZ points the gun at his own temple. His gun is jammed and simply goes "click, click, click")

Chemmed! Boy, ven things go wrong.

FRANZ sits with a sigh on the couch and drops the Luger at his side; it fires a shot.

MAX *(as he and LEO come cautiously out from under the desk and approach FRANZ)*

What were you shooting at us for us, anyway? You teutonic twit! Wait a minute, I just got an idea. A way to close the show. Franz, why don't you use this where it will do some good? Why don't you shoot the actors?

FRANZ Zee actors?

MAX Yes, zee actors. Everyone laughed at your beloved Führer tonight. Why? Because of the actors. The actors were making fun of him.

FRANZ Ja, you're right, zee actors.

MAX *(handing the Luger to FRANZ)*

Yes, here. Go. Go buy bullets. Kill. Kill all the actors.

FRANZ Yes, I must kill all zee actors.

LEO Stop! This is insanity. Have you lost your mind? How can you kill the actors? What do you mean, kill the actors? Actors are not animals, they're human beings.

MAX They are? Have you ever eaten with one?

There is the SOUND from off-stage of police whistles.

SERGEANT *(calling from off-stage right)*

All right in there, open up, it's the police!!

LEO, MAX, FRANZ The police!

LEO runs and hides unseen behind the coatrack upstage right, as MAX looks frantically around for someplace to hide but is too late. The office door bursts opens and in rushes a POLICE SERGEANT, who has a drawn gun, followed by three PATROLMEN, one of whom is black.

SERGEANT *(he speaks with a heavy New York Irish accent, as do the PATROLMEN)*

You! Drop that gun!

FRANZ Jawohl!

(he drops the gun on his foot with the cast)

Ouch!

CARMEN *(as Carmen and Roger come out of the closet)*

Officers!

SERGEANT What's going on here?

ROGER *(pointing at FRANZ)*

This crazy Kraut is crackers! He crashed in here and crassly tried to kill us!

CARMEN Oh, Roger, what alliteration!

ROGER Thank you, darling.

SERGEANT Okay, youse two can go.

ROGER AND CARMEN Thank you!

(they exit)

SERGEANT *(to one of the PATROLMEN)*

Tried to kill 'em, huh? O'Rourke, take him away. Next stop, Sing Sing!

We rewrote this scene more than any other scene in the show. We rewrote until we were dizzy. We had too much; the scene was running too long. Once "Springtime" was over, we had to get the show moving to conclusion. The last few days in Chicago, it finally came together.

We tried at least four exit lines for Franz out of the Act Two office scene. Only Chicago audiences heard Franz say, "Vy are you arresting me? I'm just a fun-loving var criminal!" Two other possibilities: "I get one phone call, ya? Does anyone know the area code for Argentina?" or "Does anyone want two dozen pigeons? They have perfect pitch!" as Franz was led away by the cop.

FRANZ Sing, Sing! Nein! You'll never take me alive!

(he runs off-stage; sounds of crashing)

SERGEANT What happened?

O'ROURKE *(from off-stage; as* MAX *mouths it)*

He broke his other leg!

SERGEANT *(to* MAX*)*

All right, now who are you and why was he trying to shoot you?

MAX *(putting on an Irish accent)*

I haven't the slightest idea, Sergeant O'Brien. The name is O'Bialystock. I was just passing by and ducked in to see what was going on. And now, with your kind permission, I'll be ducking out.

(he starts to exit)

SERGEANT Hold it! I'll decide who does the ducking here.

OFFICER O'RILEY *(having picked up the two accounting ledgers that* MAX *and* LEO *had left forgotten on the floor when* FRANZ *entered)*

Hey, Sarge, look at this.

We're ashamed to admit that we once had a run of lines in this scene involving Officer O'Riley—
Sergeant: This officer here will escort you downtown.
Max: Oh, really?
Sergeant: No, O'Riley.

We apologize. But at least we had the good taste to cut it.

SERGEANT What?

OFFICER O'RILEY I found these two accounting books on the couch. This one says, "Show to the IRS."

SERGEANT And what's the other one say?

OFFICER O'RILEY "Never show to the IRS."

SERGEANT I think the three of you better come downtown with me.

MAX Three?

SERGEANT Yeah, you and dem two books.

SERGEANT *(to the black* PATROLMAN, *who has up to now not spoken, indicating* MAX)

Officer O'Houllihan, take this mug in.

(He exits.)

O'HOULLIHAN *(with a thick Irish accent as he takes* MAX *by the arm and starts to lead him off)*

You're a lucky man, Mr. O'Bialystock; they're servin' corned beef and cabbage down to the jail tonight. Just like me darlin' mither used to make back in dear old Killarney.

MAX *(aside out front to the audience as he is led off by* O'HOULLIHAN*)*

I've heard-a black Irish, but this is ridiculous.

The stage is for a moment deserted. LIGHTS *go down and* MUSIC, *"Springtime for Hitler" in a minor key, is briefly heard.* LIGHTS *up and* MUSIC *out as* ULLA *enters in a tight-fitting and very sexy silver-lamé gown.*

ULLA Mr. Bialystock, Mr. Bloom?

A spotlight hits the coatrack, upstage left, which slowly turns to reveal LEO *hanging on it, hiding, wearing* MAX*'s oversized raincoat and with a hat over his face.*

LEO Ulla! Help me!

ULLA What happened? You hung up your coat vhile you vere still in it.

(she helps him down)

LEO Thank you for helping me down.

ULLA Vhat vere you doing?

LEO Hiding. I was hiding.

ULLA From who, from vat?

LEO The police. They were just here. They arrested Max.

ULLA Uh-oh. They found the byukes?

LEO No, no, they found the boo—yeah, the byukes, the byukes. I don't know what to do. Poor Max. Maybe I should turn myself in and go to jail with him.

ULLA Vell, my sweet cupcake, I know we both love Max, but it seems to me that you haf two choices. Number one, you can go to jail with Mr. Bialystock, for years and years and years. Or, Number two, you can take that two million dollars and Ulla and go to Rio.

At this point in the show, believe it or not, we once wrote a huge scene that took place at an outdoor nightclub on the beach in Rio, where Leo and Ulla were dancing the samba to a Mel Brooks song entitled "You'll Find Your Happiness in Rio." It got pretty crazy when conscience-stricken Leo Bloom began to see Max Bialystock's face everywhere he looked, on waitresses, cigarette girls, and finally on a Carmen Miranda-like Brazilian bombshell. This scene alone would have cost two million dollars. Thank God, it stank.

LEO Oh, my God, what a dilemma. What should I do?
Go to jail or go to Rio?

LET'S HOP A PLANE,
AND REALLY GO INSANE
IN RIO BY THE SEA.
SO IN THE END I SCREWED MY FRIEND
SO CALL IT A DISGRACE . . .

LEO AND ULLA *IT WAS WORTH IT FOR THAT FACE.*

MUSIC *instantly up: "That Face" played as a samba.* LEO *flings off the raincoat to reveal himself once again in his tuxedo, grabs* ULLA *in his arms, and they samba together around the stage and off as* LIGHTS *and* SCENERY *change, and we segue into Scene 6.*

ACT TWO - SCENE 6

A holding cell in the basement of a downtown New York City courthouse. MUSIC *under, mournfully, "The King of Broadway."*

Afternoon, a few weeks later.

MAX—*disheveled, in a wrinkled suit with his tie unknotted—is locked alone in the cell. There is nothing in the cell but a bare cot and a sink.*

MAX *(waking from a nightmare)*

No . . . No . . . Leo! Gotta think. Gotta think. Ten days and no Leo . . . Where's Leo? Ahh, what am I worrying about? He's probably on his way here right now with the best lawyer in town. I'll be outta here in time for dinner. Leo, I can always count on Leo. He must be so worried about me. Good old Leo.

A uniformed GUARD *enters carrying a piece of mail.*

GUARD Mail call! Here, Bialystock, ya got a postcard.

MAX A postcard? From where?

GUARD Brazil.

(he exits)

MAX *(examining the postcard, puzzled)*

Brazil? Who do I know in Brazil?

(reading the card aloud to himself)

Dear Max, Rio is everything you said it was and more. Ulla and I think of you every chance we get. In the morning, when we have breakfast on our terrace, many different herrings. And in the evening, when we samba together in the moonlight. Sorry, must run, Ulla's waiting, it's almost eleven. Wish you were here, Leo.

(in a rage, sings)

JUST LIKE CAIN AND ABEL,
YOU PULLED A SNEAK ATTACK

This was not the first idea we'd had for Nathan's big eleven o'clock number. Earlier, Mel had turned out a comic/sentimental ballad called "Goodbye to Broadway" that everyone agreed was terrific but not through-the-roof, not a genuine showstopping eleven o'clock number. Mel went back to the drawing board and, helped along by some Glen Kelly musical and lyric thoughts, soon came up with "Betrayed." "Thank you very much, Mel Brooks," we all instantly yelled.

I THOUGHT THAT WE WERE BROTHERS
THEN YOU STABBED ME IN THE BACK!

BETRAYED!
OH, BOY, I'M SO BETRAYED!

LIKE SAMSON AND DELILAH,
YOUR LOVE BEGAN TO FADE,
I'M CRYING IN THE HOOSEGOW,
YOU'RE IN RIO GETTING LAID!

BETRAYED!
LET'S FACE IT, I'M BETRAYED!

BOY, HAVE I BEEN TAKEN,
OY, I'M SO FORSAKEN!

I SHOULD HAVE SEEN WHAT CAME TO PASS,
I SHOULD HAVE KNOWN TO WATCH MY ASS!

I FEEL LIKE OTHELLO,
EV'RYTHING IS LOST,
LEO IS IAGO,
MAX IS DOUBLE-CROSSED!

I'M SO DISMAYED,
DID I MENTION I'M BETRAYED?!

I USED TO BE THE KING,
BUT NOW I AM THE FOOL!
A CAPTAIN WITHOUT A SHIP,
A RABBI WITHOUT A SHUL!

NOW I'M ABOUT TO GO TO JAIL,
THERE'S NO ONE WHO WILL PAY MY BAIL,
I HAVE NO ONE WHO I CAN CRY TO,
NO ONE I CAN SAY GOOD-BYE TO.

He speaks as MUSIC *continues under.*

I'm drowning! I'm drowning here! I'm going down for the last time. I see my whole life flashing before my eyes. I see a weathered old farmhouse with a white picket fence. I'm running through fields of alfalfa with my collie, Rex. Stop it, Rex! I see my mother standing on the back porch, in a worn but clean gingham gown, and I hear her calling out to me, "Alvin! Don't forget your

chores. The wood needs a-cordin' and the cows need a-milkin'. Alvin, Alvin . . . " Wait a minute! My name's not Alvin. That's not my life. I'm not a hillbilly. I grew up in the Bronx. Leo's taken everything. Even my past!

MY PAST'S A DYING EMBER,
BUT WAIT . . . NOW I REMEMBER.
HOW DID IT BEGIN?
HE WALKED INTO MY OFFICE WITH HIS COCKAMAMIE SCHEME.
YOU CAN MAKE MORE MONEY WITH A FLOP THAN WITH A HIT.
"WE CAN DO IT, WE CAN DO IT!"

(imitating LEO*)*

"I CAN'T DO IT!"

(as himself)

"WE CAN DO IT!"

(as LEO*)*

"I CAN'T DO IT!" GOODBYE, MAX!

(as himself)

LORD, I WANT THAT MONEY!

(as LEO*)*

I'M BACK, MAX!

(as himself)

"COME ON, LEO, WE CAN DO IT!"
STEP ONE, FIND THE PLAY!
SEE IT, SMELL IT, TOUCH IT, KISS IT,
HELLO, MISTER LIEBKIND.
"GUTEN TAG, HOP CLOP,
GUTEN TAG, HOP CLOP!"
ADOLF ELIZABETH HITLER?
"GUTEN TAG, HOP CLOP,
GUTEN TAG, HOP CLOP!"

STEP TWO, HIRE THE DIRECTOR.
"KEEP IT GAY, KEEP IT GAY, KEEP IT . . . "
TWO-THREE, KICK, TURN, TURN, TURN, KICK,TURN

ULLA!
OOOH WAH-WAH-WOO-WOO WAH-WAH!

STEP THREE, RAISE THE MONEY.
"ALONG CAME BIALY!"

INTERMISSION!

(several beats of total silence)

STEP FOUR, HIRE ALL THE ACTORS.
"A WANDERING MINSTREL I,
A THING OF SHREDS AND . . . "

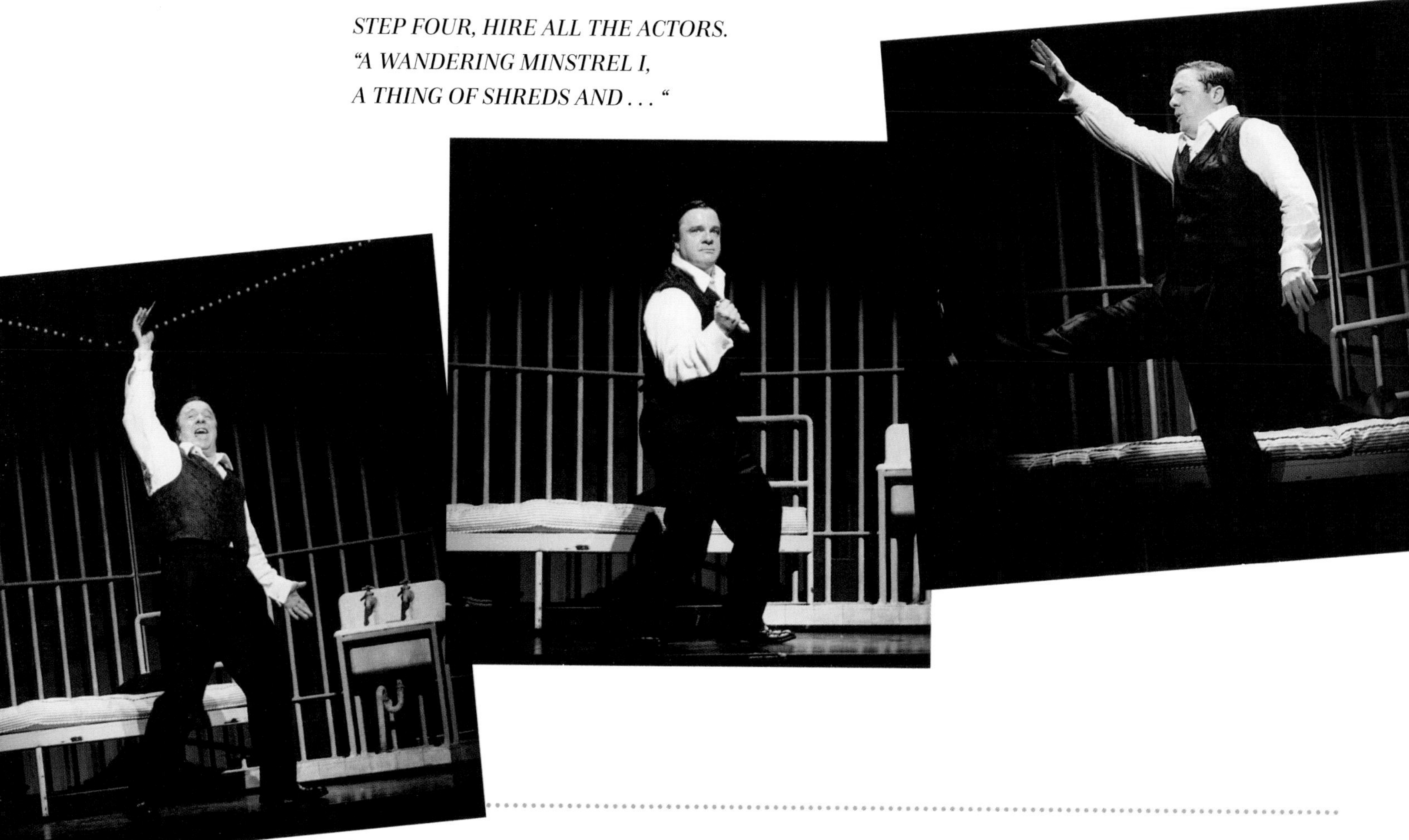

NEXT! "THE LITTLE WOODEN BOY."
NEXT! THAT'S OUR HITLER!

"OPENING NIGHT!"
GOOD LUCK, GOOD LUCK, GOOD LUCK!
BREAK A LEG! I BROKE MY LEG!

"SPRINGTIME FOR HITLER AND GERMANY!"
A SURPRISE SMASH!
"SPRINGTIME FOR HITLER AND GERMANY!
IT'LL RUN FOR YEARS!

"WHERE DID WE GO RIGHT,
WHERE DID WE GO RIGHT?"
GIMME THOSE BOOKS,
FAT, FAT, FATTY!
GIMME THOSE BOOKS,
FAT, FAT, FATTY!
BOOKS, FAT,
BOOKS, FAT,
BOOKS, FAT,
BOOKS, FAT!

LOUSY FRUIT,
KILL THE ACTORS,
YOU EVER EAT WITH ONE?!

THEN YOU RAN TO RIO
AND YOU'RE SAFELY OUT OF REACH,
I'M BEHIND THESE BARS,
YOU'RE BANGING ULLA ON THE BEACH!

JUST LIKE JULIUS CAESAR
WAS BETRAYED BY BRUTUS,
WHO'D THINK AN ACCOUNTANT
WOULD TURN OUT TO BE MY JUDAS!

I'M SO DISMAYED,
IS THIS HOW I'M REPAID,
TO BE . . .
BETRAYED!!
BETRAYED!!

As the number ends to applause, LIGHTS *and* SCENERY *change, and we segue into Scene 7.*

ACT TWO ▪ SCENE 7

A downtown New York City courtroom.

Evening, a few minutes following Scene 6.

MAX *sits at a defendant's table. A spectators' section filled with a dozen or so* LITTLE OLD LADIES, *a* DISTRICT ATTORNEY *standing next to the judge's podium, a desk for a* COURT STENOGRAPHER, *etc. A* BAILIFF *stands to one side. Presiding is* JUDGE MAXWELL, *elderly and grumpy.*

JUDGE Has the jury reached its verdict?

FOREMAN OF THE JURY Yes, we find the defendant incredibly guilty.

MAX Oy.

JUDGE Before I pass sentence, does the defendant have anything to say on his own behalf?

MAX Yes, your honor, I do. I admit, for the last twenty years, I've been a lying, double-crossing, two-faced, back-stabbing despicable crook. But I had no choice . . . I was a Broadway producer. A man without a conscience and with no one who gave a damn about him. And that, your honor, is what hurts the most. I thought that I'd at last found a loyal partner, a man who I cared about, and who I thought cared about me. And what breaks my heart is, that now, when I need him most, he's deserted me, and I will probably never see or hear from him ever again.

All fourteen of the producers of The Producers howled with laughter at these lines. Why? We weren't sure. Probably because they were ridiculously untrue. Or, on the other hand . . .

LEO *suddenly enters, in a white suit, with* ULLA, *in bright Rio resort wear, right behind him; he carries a black bag.* MUSIC: *"That Face," played as a samba.*

LEO That's not true!

LITTLE OLD LADIES, ETC. *(in shocked disbelief, upon seeing* LEO*)*

Aaahhh!

JUDGE Order in the court! Order in the court! And stop that samba!

MUSIC: *Out*

LEO I am Mr. Bialystock's partner, Leopold Bloom. A rat who deserted a sinking ship.

JUDGE I see.

(to ULLA*)*

And who are you, my dear?

ULLA My name is Ulla Inga Hansen Bensen Yonsen Tallen-Hallen Svaden-Svanson . . . Bloom.

JUDGE Bloom? You're his wife?

ULLA Ya, your honor. He vouldn't do it unless ve got married.

LEO *(stepping forward and placing the black bag on the judge's bench)*

Your Honor, this was all my scheme. I wish to turn myself in, and here is the two million dollars we stole. Minus airfare, hotels, and a large jar of cocoa butter.

JUDGE I see. Bailiff, mark this Exhibit "A."

(the BAILIFF *takes the bag and exits)*

Now, Mr. Bloom, why in God's name did you come back and give yourself up?

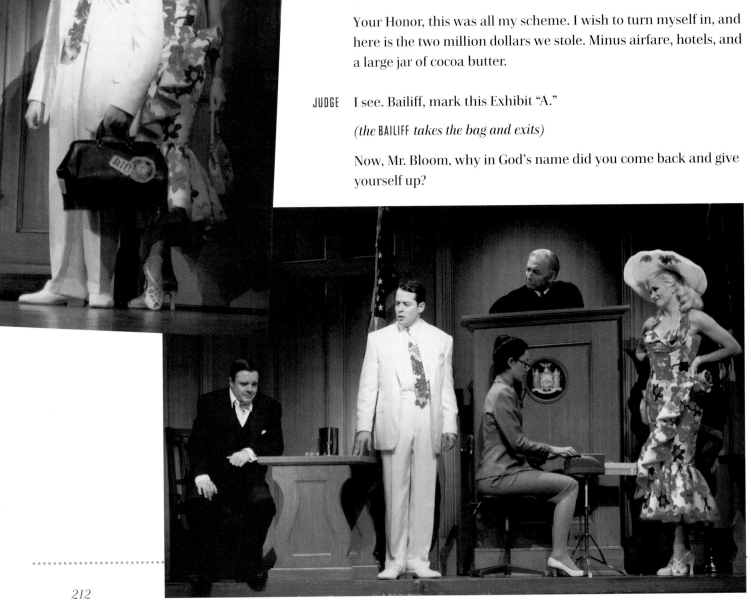

LEO Why? To speak on his behalf. To tell you what this man is really like. We all know that Max Bialystock is a lying, double-crossing, two-faced, slimy, manipulative, underhanded . . . .

MAX *(out of the side of his mouth to* LEO*)*

Please, don't help me.

LEO *(aside to* MAX*)*

Max.

MAX *(aside to* LEO*)*

What?

LEO Remember when we were on the floor fighting over the books?

MAX Yes.

LEO I'm sorry I called you fat, fat, fatty.

MAX Thank you.

LEO Your Honor, if I may address the court.

*(*MUSIC: *"'Til Him" begins under)*

As I understand it, the law was created to protect people from being wronged. So whom has Max Bialystock wronged? Not these dear ladies . . .

LITTLE OLD LADIES No.

LEO . . . And certainly not me, not me. I was this . . . nobody . . . no one ever called me Leo before. I mean, your honor, I know it isn't a big legal point, but even when I was in kindergarten, they all called me Bloom. What I'm trying to say is . . . when I was in Rio and had everything I'd ever dreamed of, I suddenly realized that . . . this man . . . this man . . .

NO ONE EVER MADE ME FEEL LIKE SOMEONE . . .
'TIL HIM.
LIFE WAS REALLY NOTHING BUT A GLUM ONE . . .
'TIL HIM.

MY EXISTENCE BORDERED ON THE TRAGIC,
ALWAYS TIMID, NEVER TOOK A CHANCE,
THEN I FELT HIS MAGIC
AND MY HEART BEGAN TO DANCE.

I WAS ALWAYS FRIGHTENED, FRAUGHT WITH WORRY . . .
'TIL HIM.
I WAS GOING NOWHERE IN A HURRY . . .
'TIL HIM.
HE FILLED UP MY EMPTY LIFE,
FILLED IT TO THE BRIM.
THERE COULD NEVER EVER BE
ANOTHER ONE . . . LIKE HIM.

MAX *(as* MUSIC *continues under)*

Leo . . . I never realized . . . you're a good singer.

LEO Thank you, Max, I sang it for you. I sang it because I'm your friend.

MAX You are? Gee, I've had a lot of relationships, but you could never call any of them friend. But come to think of it . . .

(speaking in rhythm)

. . . NO ONE EVER EVER REALLY KNEW ME . . .

(he sings, and the LITTLE OLD LADIES *join him in singing fills at appropriate points throughout the song)*

MAX	*'TIL HIM.*	LITTLE OLD LADIES	*AHH AHH AHH AHH*
	AHH		
	EVERYONE WAS ALWAYS		*AHH!*
	OUT TO SCREW ME,		
	'TIL HIM.		*AHH AHH AHH AHH!*

NEVER MET A MAN
I EVER TRUSTED,
ALWAYS DEALT WITH
SHYSTERS IN THE PAST,
NOW I'M WELL ADJUSTED,
'CAUSE I'VE GOT A FRIEND AT LAST.

(at this point, the LITTLE OLD LADIES *do an especially ornate and lengthy fill;* MAX *says, out of the side of his mouth to them, spoken)*

Don't help me.

MAX *ALWAYS PLAYING SINGLES, NEVER DOUBLES,*

	'TIL HIM.	LITTLE OLD LADIES	*OOH OHH OOH OOH*
	NEVER HAD A PAL TO		*OOHOOH!*
	SHARE MY TROUBLES,		
	'TIL HIM.		*OOH OOH OOH OOH!*

LEO *HE FILLED UP MY EMPTY LIFE, AHH AAH AAH AAH AAH AAH!*

LEO AND MAX *FILLED IT TO THE BRIM. OOH OOH OOH OOH!*

LEO *THERE COULD NEVER EVER BE ANOTHER ONE . . . LIKE HIM.*

JUDGE Gentlemen, it breaks my heart to break up such a beautiful friendship. So I won't.

(slamming down his gavel)

Five years in the state penitentiary at Sing Sing! Court adjourned!

General consternation. ULLA *and the* LITTLE OLD LADIES *scream and protest, ad lib, "No, no, please, no!"* LIGHTS *and* SCENERY *begin to change.*

MUSIC *of the introduction to "Prisoners of Love" at once begins under as Scene 7 ends.*

ACT TWO - SCENE 8

Sing Sing. A semi-abstract set, in one, with projections on the scrim, representing the prison.

As MUSIC *continues,* CONVICT #1, *in a striped prison uniform and cap, appears in a spotlight.*

Our homage, of course, genuinely heartfelt, for Hollywood's greatest movie about the movie business, Singin' in the Rain.

CONVICT #1 *GOTTA SING . . . SING!*

CONVICT #2 *(appearing in a spotlight)*

GOTTA SING . . . SING!

CONVICTS #3 AND #4 *OH, YOU CAN LOCK US UP,*
AND LOSE THE KEY,

CONVICTS # 1–4 *BUT HEARTS IN LOVE*
ARE ALWAYS FREE!

MAX All right, you animals, break's over. Let's take it from the top.

CONVICT #1 This is good! Hey, Bloom, put me down for ten grand.

CONVICTS *PRISONERS OF LOVE,*
BLUE SKIES ABOVE,
CAN'T KEEP OUR HEARTS IN JAIL!

As MUSIC *continues,* MAX, LEO, *and* FRANZ *enter in striped prison uniforms.*

MAX Tempo fellas! Pick up the tempo!

SIX CONVICTS *PRISONERS OF LOVE,*
OUR TURTLE DOVES
SOON COMING 'ROUND WITH BAIL!

MAX That's it!

LEO Sing out, boys!

SIX CONVICTS *OH, YOU CAN LOCK US UP,*
AND LOSE THE KEY,
BUT HEARTS IN LOVE
ARE ALWAYS FREE!

LEO Let 'em hear you in solitary!

PRISONERS OF LOVE,
BLUE SKIES ABOVE . . .

SIX CONVICTS *'CAUSE WE'RE STILL PRISONERS,*
WE'RE STILL PRISONERS,
WE'RE STILL PRISONERS
OF LOVE!!

MAX Take it home, boys!
We open in
Leavenworth
Saturday night!

PRISON GUARD *(racing in as* MUSIC *continues under; waving a paper in one hand)*

Bialystock, Bloom, Liebkind, good news! This just came from the governor. "Gentlemen, you are hereby granted a full pardon for having—through song and dance—brought joy and laughter into the hearts of every murderer, rapist, and sex maniac in Sing Sing." You're free!

LEO AND CONVICTS Free!

MAX Next stop, "Prisoners of Love" on Broadway!

CONVICTS Broadway! Broadway!

FRANZ I must tell my birds!

FRANZ AND CONVICTS *BUT HEARTS IN LOVE*
ARE ALWAYS FREE!

The MUSIC *of "Prisoners of Love" builds as* ULLA *and a chorus of* GIRL PRISONERS, *scantily clad in glitzy and very abbreviated Broadway versions of striped chain-gang convict uniforms, enter followed by* ROGER DE BRIS *(as a sadistic, whip-wielding* GUARD*).* ALL *sing and dance as they cross to stage center, while the scrim rises and the set changes behind them.*

ULLA AND GIRL PRISONERS *PRISONERS OF LOVE,*
BLUE SKIES ABOVE,
CAN'T KEEP OUR HEARTS IN JAIL!

ROGER *CAN'T KEEP OUR HEARTS IN JAIL!*

ULLA AND GIRL PRISONERS *PRISONERS OF LOVE,*
OUR TURTLE DOVES . . .

ROGER *SOON COMING 'ROUND WITH BAIL!*

ULLA AND GIRL PRISONERS *TOTE THAT BALE!*

MALE PRISONERS *enter in glitzy Broadway prison garb and join in.*

MALE PRISONERS *YOU CAN LOCK US UP,*
AND LOSE THE KEY,

ALL *BUT HEARTS IN LOVE*
ARE ALWAYS FREE!

We segue into Shubert Alley, as in the opening scene of the show. The marquee of the Shubert Theatre lights up, saying, "Bialystock and Bloom Present Their New Smash-hit Musical 'Prisoners of Love'!" Another sign lights up, saying, "Straight from Sing Sing—Non-Stop Laffs—A Prison Riot!" "Now in It's 4th Smash Year!"

ROGER, ULLA, AND ALL PRISONERS

PRISONERS OF LOVE,
BLUE SKIES ABOVE,
'CAUSE WE'RE STILL
PRISONERS . . .
WE'RE STILL
PRISONERS . . .
WE'RE STILL
PRISONERS OF LOVE!
LOVE!
LOVE!
LOVE!
LOVE!
LOVE!
LOVE!
LOVE!
LOVE!

ALL *exit into the Shubert,* ULLA *and* ROGER *last. Before* ROGER *can exit,* CARMEN *runs on-stage with a bouquet of roses and hands them to* ROGER. ROGER *guides* CARMEN *into the Shubert, then exits after him.* LIGHTS *and* SCENERY *change as we segue into the finale. . . .*

ACT TWO - SCENE 9

MUSIC: *Fanfare "Springtime for Hitler" into "We Can Do It" under the following.* LEO *enters from one side of the stage and* MAX *enters from the other. They meet at stage center. Both are resplendent in evening clothes. But hatless.* MAX *carries two hats, one nestled in the other.* MAX *hands a hat to* LEO, *and they both put on their matching hats at rakish angles. They shake hands.*

"Prisoners of Love" metamorphosed beautifully into "Leo and Max."

LEO AND MAX *LEO AND MAX*
UP OFF OUR BACKS,
BACK ON
THE GREAT WHITE WAY!

LEO AND MAX,
BACK ON OUR TRACKS,
WE'RE BACK
ON TOP TO STAY!

SO WHEN WE TAKE YOUR MONEY,
NEVER FEAR,
WE'LL KNOCK BROADWAY
RIGHT ON ITS EAR!

LEO AND MAX
~~BACK IN THEIR~~ WE'RE MAKING TRACKS
WATCH AS WE GO TO TOWN — CAN'T ~~KEEP~~ KEEP A ~~GREAT~~ GOOD TEAM DOWN.

TWO [GUTSY] GUYS
WE'RE ON THE RISE
~~THE TALK OF~~ TOWN
CAN'T KEE

GOING TO TOWN

WATCH AS WE

AXE
BACKS AX
BLACKS
CRACKS
FACTS FACTS
LAX ACTS
HACKS
JACKS
LACKS
KNACKS
PACKS
RACKS
TRACKS
WAX
SACKS
TACKS
TAX

THE CAST IS GREAT,
THE SCRIPT IS SWELL,
BUT THIS WE'RE TELLIN' YOU, SIRS,
IT'S JUST NO GO, YOU GOT NO SHOW,
WITHOUT THE PRODUCERS!
WE'LL NEVER QUIT,
HIT AFTER HIT . . .

MUSIC: *Fanfare "I Wanna Be a Producer" as the set parts and the logos of future Bialystock and Bloom musicals are revealed upstage, lighting up one after the other in the following order: "Maim," "Katz," "47th Street," "South Passaic," "High Button Jews," "Death of a Salesman—On Ice!" "A Streetcar Named Murray," "She Shtups to Conquer," and "Funny Boy 2."*

(as they walk arm-in-arm together into a literal sunset)

YOU AND ME-O,
WE GUARANTEE-O,
YOU'RE LOOKIN' AT
LEO AND MAX!!

ENTIRE ENSEMBLE *(off-stage)*

THE PRODUCERS,
LEO AND MAX!

CURTAIN

THE END

At the end of the bows, ALL *sing a closing song entitled "Goodbye!"*

"GOODBYE!"

ALL *THANKS FOR COMING TO SEE OUR SHOW,*
SAD TO TELL YOU WE GOT TO GO,
GRAB YOUR HAT AND HEAD FOR THE DOOR,
IN CASE YOU DIDN'T NOTICE,
THERE AIN'T ANY MORE!

IF YOU LIKE OUR SHOW TELL EV'RYONE BUT . . .
IF YOU THINK IT STINKS
KEEP YOUR BIG MOUTH SHUT!

WE'RE GLAD YOU CAME BUT WE HAVE TO SHOUT,
ADIOS, AU REVOIR, WIEDERSEHEN, TA-TA-TA,
GOODBYE . . . GET LOST . . . GET OUT!!!

When this was written, words and music both, in less than an hour one rainy afternoon in Glen Kelly's apartment, we were merely horsing around, never dreaming that it would actually end up ending the show. But Stro loved it, mainly because as a kid she'd done an all-children's show in Atlantic City that had closed with a song very similar to "Goodbye!" It became our cheerful last laugh. The cast hugely enjoys singing to their departing audiences.

Here's the song as Stro remembers it:

THANK YOU FOLKS FOR WATCHING OUR SHOW
PERFORMING FOR YOU IS A PLEASURE YOU KNOW
DO COME BACK A WEEK FROM TODAY
WHEN WE PRESENT ANOTHER CHILDREN'S TALENT DISPLAY

THANK YOU FOR DROPPING IN
IT MEANS SO MUCH TO US AS OUR CAREERS BEGIN
SO LONG, THE BEST OF LUCK TO YOU
WE'RE THE STARS OF TOMORROW TODAY

WE'RE THE STARS OF TOMORROW TODAY

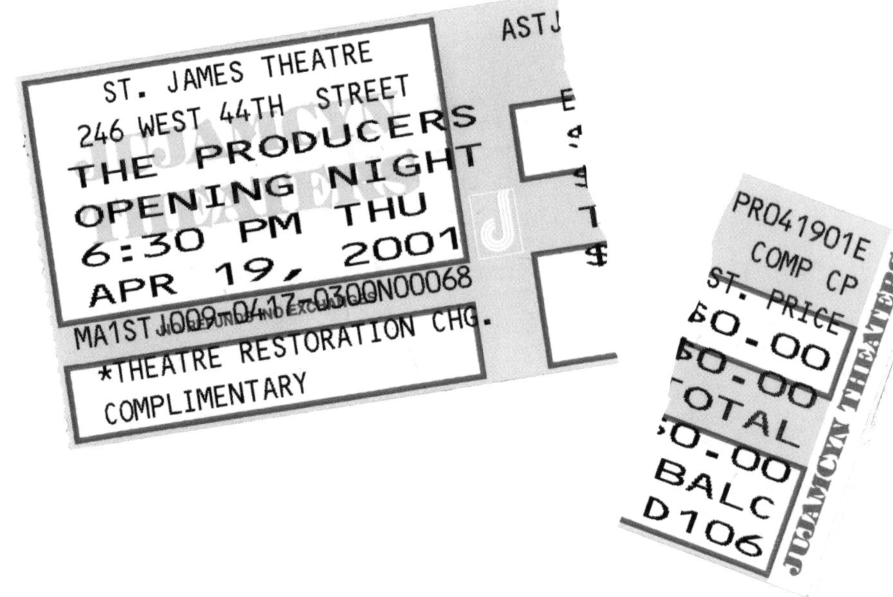

Max Bialystock
PRESENTS
THE BREAKING WIND
PRESENT
FUNNY BOY
A MUSICAL OF HAMLET
Max Bialystock
KING LEER